Y0-CCV-289

seven days battles 1862

lee's defense of richmond

ANGUS KONSTAM

seven days battles 1862

lee's defense of richmond

Praeger Illustrated Military History Series

PRAEGER

Westport, Connecticut
London

Library of Congress Cataloging-in-Publication Data

Konstam, Angus.
Seven Days Battles: Lee's defense of Richmond / Angus Konstam.
p. cm. – (Praeger illustrated military history, ISSN 1547-206X)
Originally published: Oxford: Osprey, 2004.
Includes bibliographical references and index.
ISBN 0-275-98438-9 (alk. paper)
1. Seven Days' Battles, Va., 1862. I. Title. II. Series.
E473.68.K66 2004
973.7'32–dc22 2004049505

British Library Cataloguing in Publication Data is available.

First published in paperback in 2004 by Osprey Publishing Limited, Elms Court, Chapel Way, Botley, Oxford OX2 9LP.

Library of Congress Catalog Card Number: 2004049505
ISBN: 0-275-98438-9
ISSN: 1547-206X

Praeger Publishers, 88 Post Road West, Westport, CT 06881
An imprint of Greenwood Publishing Group, Inc.
www.praeger.com

Printed in China through World Print Ltd.

The paper used in this book complies with the Permanent Paper Standard issued by the National Information Standards Organization (Z39.48-1984).

10 9 8 7 6 5 4 3 2 1

ILLUSTRATED BY: **Stephen Walsh**

CONTENTS

KEY TO MILITARY SYMBOLS

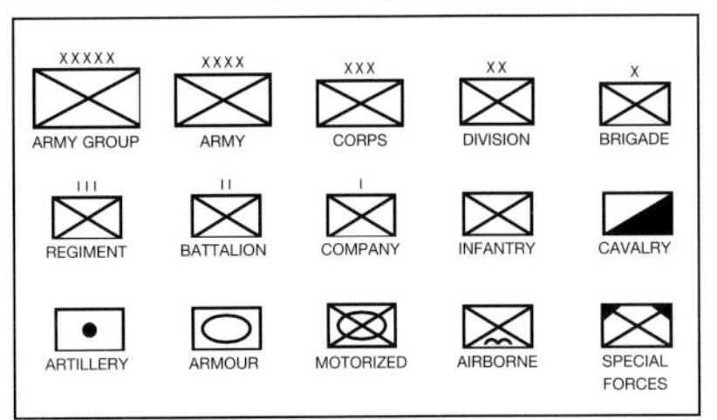

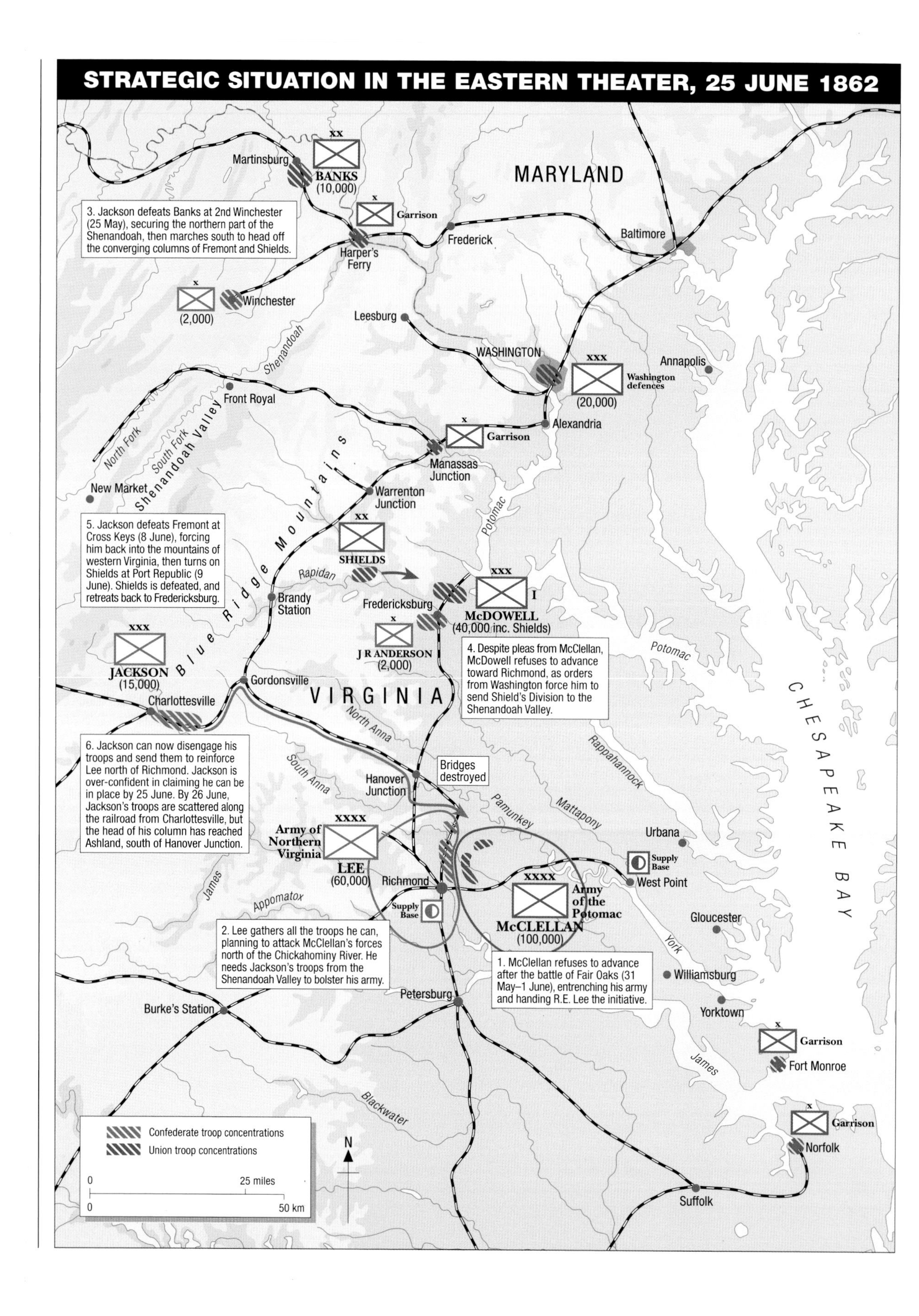
STRATEGIC SITUATION IN THE EASTERN THEATER, 25 JUNE 1862
MARYLAND
VIRGINIA
CHESAPEAKE BAY
Martinsburg
BANKS
(10,000)
Garrison
3. Jackson defeats Banks at 2nd Winchester (25 May), securing the northern part of the Shenandoah, then marches south to head off the converging columns of Fremont and Shields.
Harper's Ferry
Frederick
Baltimore
Winchester
(2,000)
Leesburg
Shenandoah
WASHINGTON
Washington defences
(20,000)
Annapolis
Front Royal
Alexandria
Garrison
Manassas Junction
North Fork
South Fork
Shenandoah Valley
New Market
Warrenton Junction
Blue Ridge Mountains
Potomac
5. Jackson defeats Fremont at Cross Keys (8 June), forcing him back into the mountains of western Virginia, then turns on Shields at Port Republic (9 June). Shields is defeated, and retreats back to Fredericksburg.
SHIELDS
Rapidan
Brandy Station
Fredericksburg
I
McDOWELL
(40,000 inc. Shields)
J R ANDERSON
(2,000)
JACKSON
(15,000)
Gordonsville
Charlottesville
4. Despite pleas from McClellan, McDowell refuses to advance toward Richmond, as orders from Washington force him to send Shield's Division to the Shenandoah Valley.
North Anna
6. Jackson can now disengage his troops and send them to reinforce Lee north of Richmond. Jackson is over-confident in claiming he can be in place by 25 June. By 26 June, Jackson's troops are scattered along the railroad from Charlottesville, but the head of his column has reached Ashland, south of Hanover Junction.
South Anna
Bridges destroyed
Hanover Junction
Rappahannock
Pamunkey
Mattapony
Urbana
Army of Northern Virginia
LEE
(60,000)
Richmond
Supply Base
West Point
Army of the Potomac
McCLELLAN
(100,000)
James
Appomatox
Supply Base
Gloucester
York
2. Lee gathers all the troops he can, planning to attack McClellan's forces north of the Chickahominy River. He needs Jackson's troops from the Shenandoah Valley to bolster his army.
1. McClellan refuses to advance after the battle of Fair Oaks (31 May–1 June), entrenching his army and handing R.E. Lee the initiative.
Williamsburg
Petersburg
Burke's Station
Yorktown
Garrison
Fort Monroe
James
Blackwater
Confederate troop concentrations
Union troop concentrations
0
25 miles
0
50 km
N
Garrison
Norfolk
Suffolk

INTRODUCTION

On 2 June 1862, Jefferson Davis, President of the Confederate States of America, ordered his military advisor, General Robert E. Lee, to take command of the Confederate forces around Richmond. The previous two months had seen the Union Army of the Potomac grinding, apparently inexorably, up the Tidewater Peninsula towards Richmond, the Southern capital. The advance had been ponderous, slowed as much by the caution of its commander, General George B. McClellan, as the actions of the defending Confederates. By late May, the Union forces were entrenched just four miles from the eastern outskirts of Richmond.

The tide of war appeared to be flowing heavily against the Confederacy. The conflict was a little over a year old, but the last Confederate victory had been at the first battle of Manassas (known in the North as Bull Run) 11 months before. Since then, there had been nothing but defeats; the fall of Forts Henry and Donelson led to the loss of western Tennessee during the winter of '61, and in April 1862 the Confederate army of General Albert S. Johnston was defeated at Shiloh, with Johnston killed in the process. The same month saw the loss of the strategically important port-city of New Orleans, while a Union naval blockade of Confederate ports was beginning to bite.

On 31 May, General Joseph Johnston launched his army into an attack against McClellan's army, which was split either side of the Chickahominy River. In two days of fighting the Confederates attempted to crush Brigadier General Keyes' IV Corps before other elements of the Army of the Potomac could come to its assistance. The battle of Fair

The objective. Richmond was more than a political symbol; it was a major manufacturing center, whose loss would cripple the Confederate war effort. In this view from the southern side of the James River the Tredegar Ironworks dominates the Richmond waterfront. (Stratford Archive)

Oaks[1] (known as Seven Pines in the North) ended in stalemate, but not before General Johnston was himself badly wounded (toward the end of the first day's fighting). It was his incapacitation that led President Davis to appoint Robert E. Lee to take command of the defense of Richmond.

This was not a popular appointment with the army, as Lee was considered too timid a commander to face the Army of the Potomac. The second major result of the battle of Fair Oaks was that General McClellan lost his nerve. Over the next two weeks, in near-incessant rain, he transferred two more army Corps to the south side of the Chickahominy River, leaving only Porter's V Corps in its original positions west of Mechanicsville. McClellan would make only one more offensive move, on 24 June, when he launched a limited assault against Brigadier General Huger's positions west of Seven Pines, the first of a series of small positional battles designed to drive the Army of Northern Virginia back toward Richmond piece by piece, and to bring the city within range of his heavy siege guns. Meanwhile, the siege guns were deployed near Gaine's Mill, on the north bank of the Chickahominy River, where they were employed sniping at Major General John Magruder's positions near the New Bridge. These were limited attacks, but not a soldier in the Army of the Potomac doubted that they presaged an advance against the Confederate fortifications in front of them. McClellan might not be the most aggressive battlefield commander, but as an engineer he understood sieges, and how to capture a city using spades, artillery and patience.

Robert E. Lee had his own plans, however, which, although they also included some digging, did not involve sitting idly while McClellan gained a stranglehold on the Southern capital. As soon as he took command of the army (which he immediately renamed the Army of Northern Virginia), he ordered the construction of a series of substantial earthworks stretching from the Chickahominy River near New Bridge to the headwaters of the White Oak Swamp. His men nicknamed him "The King of Spades" and poked fun at his apparent timidity, but these earthworks played a part in the ambitious plan he was developing. A line of fortifications could be held for some time against a superior force. Lee had no intention of passively waiting for McClellan to attack. Instead, he developed plans for one of the most ambitious offensive schemes of the war. It would ultimately save the Confederate capital and result in the utter humiliation of McClellan and his army.

1 For a more detailed analysis of the opening phases of the Peninsula Campaign and the battle of Fair Oaks/Seven Pines readers should consult Campaign Series 124 *Fair Oaks 1862 – McClellan's Peninsula campaign.*

CHRONOLOGY

1862

12 March McClellan finalizes his plans for the Peninsula Campaign.
16 March Johnston establishes his headquarters in Fredericksburg.
17 March The Army of the Potomac begins embarking at Alexandria, Virginia.
23 March Battle of Kernstown, in the Shenandoah Valley.
2 April McClellan lands at Fort Monroe.
4 April Union advance up the Peninsula begins.
5 April Union advance halted in front of Yorktown.
7 April McClellan gives the orders to prepare to besiege Yorktown.
30 April McClellan declares his siege preparations are almost complete.
3 May The Confederates abandon Yorktown.
5 May Battle of Williamsburg; Longstreet fights a successful rearguard action.
9 May Norfolk abandoned as Huger is recalled to protect Richmond.
11 May Confederate ironclad CSS *Virginia* is destroyed by her crew off Norfolk.
15 May Union ironclads repulsed by Confederate defenses at Drewry's Bluff, on the James River.
16 May McClellan establishes his new supply base at White House Landing, on the Pamunkey River.
17 May Stanton promises to release McDowell's I Corps to McClellan.
18 May McClellan reorganizes his army, creating two new Corps.
20 May McClellan establishes a bridgehead south of the Chickahominy River.
23 May Battle of Front Royal, in the Shenandoah Valley.
24 May Keyes' IV Corps ordered to deploy around Fair Oaks Station.
25 May Heintzelman's III Corps sent south of the river to support Keyes.
27 May Skirmish at Hanover Courthouse.
28 May Union cavalry destroy the rail bridge over the South Anna River.
29 May Johnston orders his divisions to concentrate in front of Richmond.
31 May Battle of Fair Oaks. Longstreet and D.H. Hill attack along the Williamsburg Road, but Whiting is late and Sumner's II Corps reaches the battlefield first. Although Keyes' Corps is virtually destroyed, Sumner and Heintzelman halt the Confederate attack. General Joseph E. Johnston is badly wounded.
1 June Longstreet resumes the attack, but is repulsed then driven back by a spirited Union counterattack south of Fair Oaks station. The battle ends in stalemate.
2 June Robert E. Lee assumes command of the Confederate Army in front of Richmond.
3 June Lee gives his command a new name – The Army of Northern Virginia.
4 June McClellan sends Franklin's Corps to reinforce Sumner and orders his army to entrench south of the river.
8 June Battle of Cross Keys results in a victory for "Stonewall" Jackson in the Shenandoah Valley.
9 June Battle of Port Republic; another victory for Jackson.
12–15 June Stuart's ride around McClellan's army.
18 June McClellan gives the precautionary order to prepare for the move of his supply base from White House Landing to Harrison's Landing.
23 June Jackson travels to Richmond to confer with Lee. He simultaneously begins the transport of his Army of the Valley from Charlottesville to Mechanicsville, in accordance with Lee's orders.
24 June Lee writes "General Order No. 75", setting in motion the Seven Days Campaign.
25 June Jackson reaches Ashland, but is well behind schedule. Lee redeploys three of his divisions, leaving Magruder and Huger facing McClellan. McClellan launches limited attack against Huger.

The Seven Days

26 June – The Battle of Mechanicsville
AM Lee and his commanders wait in vain for Jackson to arrive.
PM A.P. Hill clears the enemy from Mechanicsville, but is drawn into a frontal assault against Porter's V Corps behind Beaver Dam Creek. The assault is a bloody failure. Jackson encamps north of Porter's position.

27 June – Battle of Gaine's Mill
AM McClellan orders Porter to fall back behind Boatswain's Creek. He also gives the order to abandon White House and transport all his supplies to Harrison's Landing. North of the Chickahominy River, the Confederates march east.
PM A.P. Hill assaults Porter but is repulsed. Further attacks by Ewell and Longstreet also end in failure. However, a final attack spearheaded by units from Jackson's command and supported by D.H. Hill and Longstreet succeeds in carrying the Union position. Porter's Corps driven back in disorder, and only saved by the onset of night.

28 June – The Retreat
AM Stuart discovers the enemy have destroyed the rail bridge over the Chickahominy River. Ewell moves up in support, isolating McClellan from White House. The White House depot is abandoned, and McClellan's supply wagons safely cross the Chickahominy to the south bank.
PM Porter's V Corps and Keyes IV Corps march south toward the White Oak Bridge. The rest of the army holds the line around Fair Oaks.

This earthwork facing the Mechanicsville Bridge on the south side of the Chickahominy River was typical of the defensive works created by Lee when he assumed command of the army. (Stratford Archive)

29 June – Savage's Station

AM Franklin's VI Corps, Sumner's II Corps and Heintzelman's III Corps withdraw to Savage's Station. Magruder and Huger follow. Lee orders his army to redeploy to intercept the Army of the Potomac south of the White Oak Swamp.

PM Heintzelman and Franklin continue their retreat, leaving Sumner to hold Savage's Station. Magruder clashes with Sumner at Savage's Station. Although the battle is a stalemate, Sumner continues to withdraw after nightfall.

30 June – Frayser's Farm (Glendale)

AM Sumner, Heintzelman and Franklin deploy around Glendale crossroads. Porter and Keyes continue on towards Malvern Hill.

PM Jackson halts at the White Oak Swamp Bridge, and makes no other offensive moves that day. Huger's advance down the Charles City Road is also stalled, as is Holmes' advance down the River Road. Longstreet launches an attack toward Glendale using his own division and that of A.P. Hill. Despite being driven back, the Union line holds. The retreat continues.

1 July – Malvern Hill

AM McClellan withdraws to Harrison's Landing, leaving Porter in command at Malvern Hill. Union army secures a good defensive position.

PM The Confederates launch a series of un-coordinated assaults that are all repulsed with heavy losses. For once the entire army is committed, but can make no impression on Porter's line. Keyes' IV Corps arrives at Harrison's Landing, as does the last of McClellan's supply wagons.

1 July – Harrison's Landing

AM Porter abandons Malvern Hill during the night and continues the retreat to Harrison's Landing. Confederate army remains at Malvern Hill.

PM Stuart sent off in pursuit of the Union army.

2 July The last of the Army of the Potomac reaches the safety of Harrison's Landing. Stuart arrives, but decides the position is impregnable. His artillery fires the last rounds of the campaign. Lee declares 2 July as the official end of the Seven Days campaign.

8 July Lee's army returns to Richmond.

11 July Halleck appointed as new Commander in Chief of the Union Army.

12 July Lee sends Jackson to Gordonsville.

14 July Banks ordered to advance down the Shenandoah toward Gordonsville

16 July Burnside's IX Corps arrives at Fort Monroe after garrisoning North Carolina coast.

18 July Pope decides to reinforce McDowell along the Rappahannock River.

19 July Halleck orders Burnside to reinforce Pope rather than McClellan.

27 July Meeting between McClellan and Halleck at Harrison's Landing. Lee sends A.P. Hill to join Jackson.

3 August McClellan ordered to abandon Harrison's Landing, and sail to reinforce Pope near Manassas.

5 August Burnside arrives at Fredericksburg.

8 August Pope concentrates around Culpeper Courthouse.

9 August Battle of Cedar Mountain. Banks defeated by Jackson.

17–24 August Pope and Lee concentrate their forces on the Rappahannock.

24–27 August Lee orders his army to march behind Pope to reach Manassas.

29–30 August Battle of Second Manassas (Bull Run). Confederate victory.

OPPOSING PLANS

Robert E. Lee was faced with a difficult operational problem. He had managed to gather together an army of around 70,000 men in front of Richmond. Jackson's Army of the Valley could be called upon to reinforce the Army of Northern Virginia if Lee requested it, as could Holmes' Division from the Division of North Carolina. This would give Lee something akin to parity of numbers with McClellan's Army of the Potomac, which he estimated to number around 110,000 men. Of these, substantial detachments were deployed to protect the Union lines of supply, and spies reported that the incidence of sickness within the Union army was increasing, mainly as it was camped close to the malarial waters of the Chickahominy River and the White Oak Swamp.

After the battle of Fair Oaks (31 May–1 June), McClellan redeployed his forces so that only Porter's V Corps was left on the northern bank of the Chickahominy River. On 12 June, J.E.B. Stuart led his Confederate cavalry in a spectacular ride around McClellan's army, crossing the Richmond & York River Railroad at Tunstall's Station, then fording the Chickahominy River close to its confluence with the James River. While this escapade raised morale in the Confederate camp, it also provided Lee with some valuable information. The most significant discovery was that apart from a screen of cavalry under the command of General Stoneman, no Union troops were deployed north of Porter's right flank

Colonel Bradley T. Johnson's 1st Maryland Regiment at the battle of Gaine's Mill. During the final assault the regiment began to waver. Johnson halted his regiment while under heavy fire, dressed its ranks then led it forward with the rest of Ewell's Division. (Maryland Historical Society, Baltimore, MD)

During the final stages of the battle of Gaine's Mill many of Porter's guns fired as long as they could, then their crews joined the retreat. As most of the horse teams were killed the gunners were unable to save their guns. (Stratford Archive)

near Mechanicsville. As the rest of the Union army lay south of the Chickahominy River, this meant that only one Union Corps lay between Lee and the Union supply base at White House, on the Pamunkey River. McClellan was dependent on this base, and the railroad line running southwest from it, to supply his army via his forward railhead at Savage's Station. In order to invest Richmond McClellan would probably rely on his siege train, as had been the case in front of Yorktown. While the more mobile of these huge naval guns could be brought forward by wagons, the majority could only be transported by either sea or rail. As there was no landing place close to the army, the railroad was the only means of transporting this ordnance. Clearly if the railroad could be cut, McClellan would be trapped on the southern bank of the Chickahominy River, and would have to come out of his entrenchments, cross the river in the face of Confederate fire, and fight a battle for control of his supply line. If he lost this battle, the Army of the Potomac would be all but destroyed. It was a bold vision, made all the more appealing when news reached Richmond that Jackson's Army of the Valley had defeated the last Union forces in the Shenandoah Valley. If Jackson could be transported to Richmond, then the combined weight of Lee and Jackson should be enough to annihilate Porter and then cut McClellan's lifeline.

Lee's plan was one of great daring, and could even be construed as reckless. Since early June, the two armies had constructed a series of field fortifications running southward from the Chickahominy River to the White Oak Swamp. The information supplied by Stuart told Lee that McClellan had concentrated four of his five Corps in this fortified area. In order to put Lee's plan into effect the bulk of the Army of Northern Virginia would have to slip away from these entrenchments and re-deploy where they could storm Porter's positions on the northern bank of the river. Clearly this meant leaving the field fortifications in front of Richmond with a force that was significantly smaller than the total of the Union troops facing them. The danger was that while Lee was concentrating his force north of the river, McClellan could launch an

Colonel Hiram Berdan's 1st US Sharpshooters were attached to Porter's V Corps. At Malvern Hill they were deployed in support of Porter's gun line, and inflicted heavy casualties through their accurate long-range rifle fire. (Stratford Archive)

assault south of the Chickahominy, which given the disparity in numbers would almost certainly result in a Union breakthrough. This meant the destruction in detail of a sizeable portion of the Confederate army, the fall of Richmond, and the isolation of Lee's remaining troops north of the city, where they would be cut off from their lines of communication and supply. At the start of the summer, many soldiers on both sides regarded Lee as a cautious, even timid, commander. The campaign that followed would dispel any such assumption. It was an immense gamble, and employed against a more able opponent the plan might have gone horribly wrong. Lee was counting on McClellan to remain as cautious as he had been so far in the Peninsula. He also relied on the plan remaining a secret. Given hard intelligence of the coming offensive, even McClellan might be tempted to storm Richmond's defenses.

His first problem was Jackson. Called to Richmond for a secret meeting, Jackson informed Lee that his army could be in position near Mechanicsville on 25 June. This involved moving his army from the Shenandoah to Richmond by rail and foot, as the railroad ended at the South Anna River, where Union raiders had destroyed the bridges. The Virginia Central Railroad ran from Staunton at the southern end of the Shenandoah Valley through Charlottesville and Gordonsville before heading east for 40 miles to Hanover Junction. There Jackson's men would have to disembark, then cross the South Anna to Ashland, and from there march toward Mechanicsville. It was a tall order, but Jackson and his men had established a reputation for fast movement, and although there was insufficient rolling stock available to move the whole Valley army at once, Jackson proposed running a shuttle between Charlottesville and Hanover Junction. Jackson then intimated that his men were already on their way from Charlottesville. The matter was settled. Jackson would be available to help Lee drive McClellan from Richmond.

Lee outlined his plan to President Jefferson Davis, who was naturally concerned over the risk to his capital. Then General Whiting gave a presentation, explaining with mathematical precision exactly what would happen if Lee did nothing. With his superior numbers and siege guns McClellan could afford to fight a positional battle, capturing one portion of the Confederate line, then another. By this means he could slowly push the Confederates back, using his siege guns to counter any attempt to prevent his progress. The only viable solution was Lee's offensive strategy, so President Davis had little choice but to concur with his general.

The details were finally worked out. The small commands of John Magruder (six brigades) and Benjamin Huger (three brigades), 25,000 men in total, would remain in the Richmond earthworks, facing McClellan, who Lee estimated had three times that number of men south of the Chickahominy River. Lee would then concentrate his main striking force – the three divisions of Longstreet, A.P. Hill and D.H. Hill south of the river – immediately opposite the Union-held hamlet of Mechanicsville. At the appointed moment these troops would cross the river and assault Porter's position. The real icing on the cake was to be Jackson. If he could move into place to the north and east of Mechanicsville by the time the offensive was due to begin, Lee could pin Porter in his earthworks while Jackson worked round behind the Union commander to fall on his Corps from the flank and rear. The result would be a slaughter, and would open the way to White House. Lee's other concern was intelligence. Stuart returned from his raid on 15 June, some 10 days before the assault was due to begin. Could McClellan have got wind of the operation, or of the redeployment of Jackson, and sent one or more Corps to reinforce Porter? In all written orders, Lee referred to "the enemy" north of the river, rather than "V Corps". This was because he didn't know exactly what he might be facing once the attack began. His one advantage is that he had learned from the newspapers that McClellan was unsure of Confederate numbers. This might make him timid enough to avoid attacking Richmond while Lee prepared to spring his trap.

The plan was formulated in Lee's "General Order No. 75", drafted on 24 June. To summarize the plan, it called for Jackson *"to proceed tomorrow from Ashland towards the Slash Church and encamp at some convenient point west of the Central Railroad ..."* Branch's Brigade of A.P. Hill's Division would be deployed at Half Sink as a link between the two commands. Then *"At 3 'o'clock Thursday morning, 26th instant, General Jackson will advance on the road leading to Pole Green Church, communicating his march to General Branch ..."* As soon as Branch brought word that Jackson was ready, A.P. Hill would *"move direct upon Mechanicsville,"* supported by artillery on the south side of the river. Once Mechanicsville was cleared and the Mechanicsville Bridge unmasked, Longstreet and D.H. Hill would cross to the north bank, then deploy in echelon and *"endeavor to drive the enemy from his position ... General Jackson, bearing well to his left, turning Beaver Dam Creek and taking the direction toward Cold Harbor. They will then press forward to the York River Railroad, closing upon the enemy's rear and forcing him down the Chickahominy."* Clearly the plan relied on Jackson to turn the enemy's flank, and then for the rest of the army to speed down the road toward the railroad before McClellan knew what was happening. What followed were two pieces of sheer optimism: *"Any advance of the enemy towards Richmond will be prevented by vigorously following his rear and crippling and arresting his progress."* Even more optimistically it said: *"The divisions under Generals Huger and Magruder will hold their positions ... and make demonstrations Thursday as to discover his operations. Should opportunity offer, the feint will be converted into a real attack."* Stuart was then ordered to deploy on the left of Jackson and wait for further orders. Success depended on several factors; Union weakness north of the river, the timidity of McClellan, the ability of Jackson to move into place, and the success of the initial attacks at Mechanicsville. It was a superbly imaginative plan, worthy of a general who was willing to gamble everything on winning a victory. However, there was also a lot that could go wrong.

OPPOSING COMMANDERS

Major General George B. McClellan (1826–85) was convinced his Army of the Potomac was heavily outnumbered by Robert E. Lee's Army of Northern Virginia, and consequently, through his defeatism, he became as much an architect of his own defeat as Lee was. (United States Military Academy, West Point, NY)

UNION

Major General George Brinton McClellan (1826–85)

A Philadelphian, McClellan graduated from West Point in 1846 and became a lieutenant in the engineers. He served with distinction during the Mexican-American War (1846–48), emerging with the brevet rank of Colonel. In 1855 he traveled to Europe as part of a US military delegation charged with observing the Crimean War (1854–56), and on his return he published his findings in a book entitled *The Armies of Europe.* He resigned his commission in 1857 to accept a more lucrative post as the Chief Engineer on the Illinois State Railroad. By 1860 his genius for administration saw him rise to become the President of the Ohio and Mississippi Railroad Company. When the war began McClellan was offered a commission as Major General of the Ohio State Volunteers. His performance in Western Virginia (now West Virginia) earned him a commission as Major General in the regular army, and gained him recognition in Washington. Lincoln then named McClellan commander of the Washington defenses. He subsequently replaced General Winfield Scott as the commander of the US Army. One of his tasks was to transform the army that had been defeated at First Manassas (Bull Run) in July 1861 into a fighting force. He christened this formation the "Army of the Potomac", and spent the rest of the year turning this raw amateur army into a well-trained force with the will to win, and the supplies and equipment it needed to ensure victory. Almost single-handedly, McClellan built the army that would eventually capture Richmond and ensure the defeat of the Confederacy. Unfortunately for McClellan, it was not to do so with him at its head.

He was a popular commander, with the confidence of his men, dubbed "Little Mac" by his men and "Young Napoleon" by the press. Unfortunately his military prowess was less than Napoleonic in scale. After a winter of inaction (for which he was roundly criticized by both politicians and newsmen), McClellan launched his new campaign in the spring of 1862. In a bold move he transported his army down to Fort Monroe, on the tip of Virginia's Tidewater Peninsula. Once in the field he proved an incredibly cautious commander, spending a month investing Yorktown, and two months reaching the outskirts of Richmond. All the time he complained he had insufficient men, and carped about the lack of support he enjoyed in Washington. In the hands of anyone else the Army of the Potomac could have bludgeoned its way into Richmond that summer. Instead McClellan ran out of steam on the outskirts of the city, and surrendered the initiative to his opponents. His army was attacked and almost defeated at Fair Oaks (31 May–1 June 1862), and after that McClellan remained on the defensive, apart from launching small positional attacks south of the Chickahominy River. In effect he allowed Lee to dominate the course of the campaign. During the campaign McClellan rarely showed any form of leadership, and became obsessed with the need to save his army and move his supply base. The result was a disastrous performance, redeemed only by the skill shown by the men of the army and by some of his subordinate commanders.

After the humiliation of the Seven Days, McClellan somehow retained his command, although he never regained the confidence of either his men or his superiors in Washington. After an equally lack-luster performance at Antietam he was removed from command.

Brigadier General Edwin V. Sumner (1797–1863) commanded II Corps during the Peninsula campaign. His gritty defense at Savage's Station bought time to save the army's wounded, but this was nullified by McClellan's orders to retreat. (Library of Congress)

Brigadier General Edwin Vose Sumner (1797–1863), commander of II Corps

A native of Boston, Sumner entered service with the cavalry on the western frontier, and then commanded the army's cavalry school. As a Major he commanded the 2nd US Dragoon Regiment during the Mexican-American War (1846–48), and won glory with a successful charge at the battle of Molina del Ray. After the war he served as the military governor of the New Mexico Territory and of Kansas, before becoming the commander of the Army's Department of the West. When the war began Sumner was called to Washington, where he helped McClellan build his new army. In May 1862 he was given command of II Corps. Sumner displayed initiative during the battle of Fair Oaks, and successfully took charge of the battle on the second day of fighting.

During the Seven Days campaign he displayed a similar level of initiative during the battles of Savage's Station and Frayser's Farm, making him one of the more successful Corps commanders in the army. He continued to command his Corps until his death from congestion of the lungs in March 1863.

Brigadier General Samuel Peter Heintzelman (1805–80), the commander of III Corps masterminded the determined Union defense at Frayser's Farm (Glendale), when he stopped a spirited attack by Longstreet. (Library of Congress)

Brigadier General Samuel Peter Heintzelman (1805–80), commander of III Corps

A German Pennsylvanian, Heintzelman graduated from West Point in 1826, then served in the infantry in Florida and Mexico. Promoted following conspicuous service during the Mexican-American War (1846–48), Heintzelman then served on the Western frontier and in Texas before his recall to Washington in April 1861. He was duly promoted to Lieutenant Colonel and given command of the 17th US Infantry. Within two months he was promoted to Brigadier General of Volunteers, and subsequently commanded a division during the First Manassas campaign. In March 1862, Heintzelman was given command of III Corps, a post he held throughout the Peninsula campaign. He fought well at Williamsburg and Fair Oaks, but his real test came during the Seven Days campaign, when he commanded the Union defenses around Frayser's Farm. A skilled rather than a gifted soldier, he continued to command III Corps through the Second Manassas campaign. During the Antietam (Sharpsburg) campaign his III Corps remained in the Washington defenses. On 12 October 1862, he was relieved of Corps command and assigned to the Military District of Washington, remaining in the capital for almost two years. He ended the war in command of the Northern Department headquartered at Columbus, Ohio.

Brigadier General Fitz-John Porter (1822–1901) and his V Corps bore the brunt of the fighting during the Seven Days, and in the process he displayed his abilities as a gifted defensive commander. (Library of Congress)

Brigadier General Erasmus Darwin Keyes (1810–95), commander of IV Corps

The Massachusetts-born Keyes graduated from West Point in 1832, and then served in the artillery. After serving in the South, he joined the staff of General Winfield Scott as a military secretary, advising his commander on the situation on the Western frontier. He taught artillery tactics at West Point during the 1850s, and then rejoined General Scott's staff shortly before the war began. In June 1861, he became a Brigadier General of Volunteers, and the following month he commanded a brigade with distinction during the battle of First Manassas (Bull Run). In March 1862, President Lincoln named him commander of IV Corps, and he retained this command throughout the Peninsula campaign. He bore the brunt of Johnston's attack at Fair Oaks on 31 May, and although he performed well enough during the battle, his corps was badly shattered. He played a minor role in the Seven Days campaign, as his depleted Corps remained south of the Chickahominy River, and then was the first to be withdrawn to Harrison's Landing when the retreat began.

When McClellan withdrew his army from the Peninsula, Keyes remained behind to command the Union troops who garrisoned the lower Peninsula. He resigned from the army in 1864, and then moved to California where he became a successful businessman.

Brigadier General Fitz-John Porter (1822–1901), commander of V Corps

Born in Portsmouth, New Hampshire, Porter was the son of a distinguished naval officer, whose uncle won renown as a naval commander during the War of 1812. He was also a cousin of David D. Porter, a Union Admiral who served with distinction during the Civil War. Surprisingly he opted for a career in the army rather than the navy, and graduated from West Point in 1845. He won two brevet promotions for gallantry during the Mexican-American War (1846–48), and then served as an instructor and adjutant at West Point until 1855. He took part in a military expedition in Utah during the years preceding the war, and following the commencement of hostilities he served as a staff officer in the east, organizing the recruitment of volunteers. On 14 May 1861, he was promoted to the rank of Colonel in the regular army and given command of an old regular regiment of infantry. However promotion soon followed, and he became first a Brigadier General of Volunteers and then received command of a Division in the Army of the Potomac. During McClellan's reorganization of the army in May 1861, Porter was given command of the newly constituted V Corps, the largest formation in the army. This promotion was largely due to his loyal support of McClellan and, despite his superb performance during the Seven Days campaign, Porter's fate remained entwined with that of McClellan. He handled his Corps well during the defensive battles of Mechanicsville and Gaine's Mill, and he repeated this performance at Malvern Hill, where he effectively ran the battle on behalf of his absent friend and commander.

Major General William B. Franklin (1823–1903) played a minor role in the campaign, although his VI Corps was involved in the fighting at Frayser's Farm and White Oak Swamp. (Stratford Archive)

Major General William B. Franklin (1823–1903), commander of VI Corps

At West Point, Franklin graduated first in the class of 1841 – Ulysses S. Grant graduated 21st in the same class. He served with the infantry during the Mexican-American War and then held a string of administrative commands until the outbreak of the Civil War, when he was commissioned as the Colonel of the 12th US Infantry. Three days later he was named a Brigadier General of Volunteers, and commanded a brigade with mixed fortunes during the First Manassas campaign. A faithful supporter of McClellan, he began the Peninsula campaign as a Divisional commander, but his zeal and loyalty were rewarded with command of VI Corps when McClellan reorganized his army. He fought well during the Seven Days campaign, his greatest test coming at Frayser's Farm, when he fed reinforcements into the battle, helping to stall Longstreet's attack. After the campaign he retained command of his Corps to participate in the Antietam campaign, but criticism of his performance at Fredericksburg in December 1862 led to his removal from active command. After the war he became the manager of the Colt Firearms factory in his native Connecticut.

General Robert E. Lee (1807–70) devised the audacious plan that would sweep McClellan's Union army from the gates of Richmond. Although the campaign did not unfold as he expected, his gift for improvization ensured that the Army of the Potomac would endure a humiliating strategic defeat. Painting by James A. Elder (Washington and Lee University, Lexington, VA).

CONFEDERATE

General Robert E. Lee (1807–70)

Born the son of American Revolutionary War hero "Light Horse Harry Lee", the young Virginian graduated from West Point in 1829, the same year he married Mary Custis, a granddaughter of George Washington. Lee joined the engineers, and spent the next decade in Washington and New York, or surveying fortifications and rivers in the Mississippi Delta and along the Atlantic seaboard. During the Mexican-American War, Lee distinguished himself in several battles, earning the recognition of his superiors, although he was wounded at the battle of Chapultepec outside Mexico City. He ended the war as a brevet Colonel and then served as the Superintendent at West Point until 1855. He was then assigned to the 2nd US Cavalry, and served on the western frontier under Colonel Albert Sydney Johnston, who was subsequently killed at Shiloh. Lee was stationed in Washington during 1859, and was ordered to quell the abolitionist rising at Harper's Ferry led by John Brown. Lee forced Brown's surrender, and was rewarded by a promotion and an appointment to Texas. He was recalled to Washington in early 1861, when he was offered command of the Union Army. With regret he declined the offer, then returned to his home in Arlington to write his letter of resignation. His first loyalty was to the Commonwealth of Virginia. He resigned his commission on 25 April 1861, and a month later he was commissioned into the Confederate army.

During 1861, Lee served in the Department of Georgia, South Carolina and Florida, where he improved the region's coastal defenses. After a less than glorious foray into Western Virginia, where he briefly held an independent command, Lee was recalled to Richmond, becoming military advisor to President Davis. Following the wounding of General Joseph E. Johnston at Fair Oaks, Lee was appointed as the new commander of the Confederate army in front of Richmond. The following day he gave it the new, and soon to be legendary, name of the "Army of Northern Virginia". Lee retained command of the army throughout the war, through all its trials and victories – the Seven Days battles, Antietam, Fredericksburg, Chancellorsville, Gettysburg, the Wilderness, Petersburg – ultimately

Major General Thomas J. "Stonewall" Jackson (1824–63) may have been regarded as a hero after his brilliant campaign in the Shenandoah Valley, but during the Seven Days his performance was worse than mediocre. (Stratford Archive)

surrendering his command to the Federal Commander in Chief, General Ulysses S. Grant, at Appomattox.

During the Seven Days campaign Lee out-maneuvered and out-thought McClellan, but he was consistently led down by poor staff work and a lack of detail. Both errors would be rectified during the months that followed. His strategic plan was sound, and Lee displayed considerable ability as he reconfigured this plan in the wake of McClellan's unexpected retreat and change of supply base. Today Lee is an idol of the South, and his military reputation is vigorously defended. However, even his staunchest supporter has to question his ability to control his subordinates and his army during the Seven Days battles. This lack of control allowed McClellan to escape annihilation, and robbed Lee of the chance to end the war that summer.

Major General Thomas J. "Stonewall" Jackson (1824–63)

Born in Clarksburg, Virginia (now West Virginia), Jackson had an unhappy childhood. His father died when he was two, and his mother remarried four years later. Her new husband took a dislike to her children, so the young Jackson left home to be raised by his uncle. He entered West Point in 1842 and graduated four years later, at which point he joined the artillery. Jackson served in the Mexican-American War, and ended the war as a brevet Major. In 1851, he resigned his commission to take up a teaching appointment at the Virginia Military Institute (VMI) in Lexington, and two years later he married, although his wife died in 1854 giving birth to their stillborn child. Jackson remarried, but his academic life ended when war was declared. Jackson was placed in charge of the VMI's cadets, but by June 1861, he received a commission as a Brigadier General. He commanded this brigade at the battle of First Manassas (Bull Run) in July 1861, and his steady defense on Henry House Hill earned him the nickname "Stonewall", a name first coined by Brigadier General Bee, who pointed out to his men how Jackson stood his ground "like a stone wall." He was then appointed to command the Confederate forces in the Shenandoah Valley, and after a mediocre start, he won a string of battles during the spring and early summer of 1862; Front Royal, Winchester, Cross Keys, and Port Republic. His victories in the Shenandoah Valley were achieved at great odds, and established his reputation as one of the greatest commanders of the war. Today his Valley Campaign of 1862 is regarded as a classic example of defensive strategy against a superior enemy. When Lee summoned Jackson and his "Army of the Valley" to Richmond his reputation was high.

During the Seven Days campaign Jackson displayed none of his characteristic zeal and alacrity, and can even be held responsible for a string of lost opportunities at Mechanicsville, Gaine's Mill, Savage's Station, White Oak Swamp, and Frayser's Farm. His movements were tardy, he seemed confused over his orders, and he let the enemy escape his clutches, all of which were contrary to everyone's expectation of this firebrand general. He was actually suffering from chronic fatigue, and clearly this impaired his judgment. Unable to function properly, it would have been better to hand over his command and recover his health. Instead he emerged from the campaign with a tarnished reputation, and he even tried to tender his resignation in the weeks that followed. Lee gave him a second chance, and by the following month he was back to his old form, running circles around Pope in central Virginia. He went on to become Lee's most trusted lieutenant, and played a major part in the fighting at Antietam, Fredericksburg, and Chancellorsville, where he was accidentally killed by his own troops. While "Stonewall" now enjoys a reputation second only to Lee, the best that can be said of his performance during the Seven Days was that this was not his finest hour.

Major General James Longstreet (1821–1904) proved his abilities as a senior commander during the campaign, and his attacks at Gaine's Mill and Frayser's Farm were both aggressive and effectual. (Valentine Museum, Richmond. VA)

Major General James Longstreet (1821–1904)

Born in Edgefield, South Carolina, Longstreet graduated from West Point in 1842 and joined the infantry. He distinguished himself during the Mexican-American War, and emerged as a brevet Major. He served as a paymaster until he resigned his commission in June 1861. Commissioned as a Brigadier General, he saw service at First Manassas (21 July 1861), and was promoted to the rank of Major General the following October. He won a defensive victory at Williamsburg, his performance earning him the chance to act as a de-facto Corps commander during the battle of Fair Oaks (31 May–1 June 1862). His attack was spirited although his deployment was somewhat mismanaged, and when Lee assumed command he seemed wary of Longstreet, who resumed the duties of a divisional commander. A religious man, his once jovial demeanor was crushed by the death of his two children in 1862, so to strangers he appeared taciturn and aloof.

During the Seven Days, Longstreet was on better form, making a series of skillfully handled attacks at Gaine's Mill, then launching an assault that almost broke the Union defenses at Frayser's Farm. During the battle of Malvern Hill he acted as Lee's understudy as his commander was somewhat incapacitated, but he seemed unable to direct the battle that followed with any real effect. However, Longstreet emerged from the campaign with a reputation for being a gifted fighter, and he went on to serve as a one of Lee's trusted Corps commanders at Antietam, Fredericksburg, Chancellorsville, Gettysburg, and beyond. Following Jackson's death at Chancellorsville, Longstreet continued to serve as Lee's principal lieutenant until the final surrender at Appomattox in April 1865.

Brigadier General John Bankhead Magruder (1807–71), nicknamed "Prince John", emerged from the campaign with a largely undeserved reputation for tardiness and lack of aggression because of his performance at Savage's Station. (Louisiana State University Library, Baton Rouge, LA)

Brigadier General John Bankhead Magruder (1807–71)

Born in Winchester, Virginia, Magruder graduated from West Point in 1830, and then served in the 7th US Infantry. He soon transferred to the artillery, and served on garrison duty on the Atlantic seaboard before his participation in the Seminole War in Florida (1837–38) and the Mexican-American War. He emerged from the war as a brevet Colonel. For the next decade he served in various coastal fortifications and frontier posts until he resigned his commission when Virginia seceded from the Union.

Magruder earned the nickname "Prince John" because of his flamboyant social life and his elegant appearance, often living beyond his means. He was also a gifted soldier, and President Davis made him a Brigadier General. During the early stages of the Peninsula campaign he commanding the Confederate forces around Yorktown, and his superb deceptions fooled McClellan into thinking Magruder commanded a far larger force than he actually had. Consequently McClellan prepared a

Lee's dashing cavalry commander, Brigadier General J.E.B. Stuart (1833–64), provided the intelligence his commanding officer needed to plan the offensive to drive the Union army from Richmond. Painting by Cornelius Hankins (Virginia Historical Society, Richmond, VA)

formal siege of Yorktown, and Magruder bought the Confederates a month in which to organize the defense of Richmond. His deception probably saved Richmond and the Confederacy. During the Seven Days battles, Lee came to question his aggression at Savage's Station, although Magruder seemed aggressive enough at Malvern Hill, when he led several unsuccessful attacks against the Union lines. After the campaign was over Magruder was posted to Texas, where he assumed command of Confederate forces in the far west.

Major General Benjamin Huger (1805–77)

Benjamin Huger was born into a military family from Charleston, South Carolina, and it was inevitable he would go to West Point. He graduated in 1825 then joined the artillery, spending three years working as a topographer before his appointment as an ordnance officer in 1828. For the next 12 years he ran the armory in Fort Monroe, then served on the War Department's Ordnance Board. During the Mexican-American War, Huger became General Winfield Scott's Chief of Ordnance, receiving several brevets for his services. Between the two wars he developed new artillery tactics and advised the War Department on ordnance, but when Virginia seceded he resigned his commission, becoming a Brigadier General in the Confederate army. Over the next year he was defeated at Roanoke Island and then forced to surrender Norfolk in order to reinforce Johnston's army in front of Richmond. His reputation was therefore questionable, and his performance during the Fair Oaks campaign did little to improve it. During the Seven Days campaign Huger helped Magruder defend Richmond, then bungled his part in the pursuit of the Union army. His lackluster performance led to his removal from active duty, and he subsequently served as an ordnance inspector before being shipped off to the Trans-Mississippi Department.

OPPOSING ARMIES

THE UNION ARMY

A Confederate Infantryman photographed at the start of the war. Like many of the Confederate soldiers who participated in the Seven Days battles, he wears a uniform supplied from the Richmond Depot. (Stratford Archive)

The nature of both armies during this campaign has already been described in Campaign 124 *Fair Oaks 1862 – McClellan's Peninsula campaign*, which allows us to concentrate on changes that affected the army after the battle of Fair Oaks (31 May–1 June). Major General McClellan's Army of the Potomac was a superb military tool, and in the right hands it should have been the "unstoppable and invincible force" which it had been dubbed by the press and by soldiers alike. In the 3½ weeks following the battle, McClellan did little apart from complain to Washington that he had insufficient troops, concentrated his forces in the area of Fair Oaks (where he anticipated another assault would be made), and ordered the digging of vast lines of entrenchments.

Betrayed by his intelligence services and by his own innate caution, McClellan became convinced that he was heavily outnumbered. Even after the Seven Days campaign began, he explained his reverses to Washington by stating that the outcome would have been different if he had been given another 10,000 or 20,000 troops. If he really believed he faced a Confederate army of over 200,000 men, this small addition would have made little difference to the outcome of the campaign. Rather, it was a device he used to berate Secretary of War Stanton and Lincoln, who deprived him of the use of BrigGen Irvin McDowell's I Corps. In fact the troops he actually had at his disposal in the Virginia Peninsula were ample for the task in hand. An army return of 20 June was sent to Washington from McClellan's headquarters. It listed the entire strength of the Army of the Potomac, dividing them into "aggregate present and absent", "aggregate present", and "present for duty, equipped". The last figure is the most important, and although this reduces McClellan's available strength by around 25,000 men, it still leaves him with a total of 114,691 men. From this we can determine roughly how many men he had available at the start of the campaign some six days later. The garrison of Brigadier General Silas Casey at White House Landing (4,505 men) can be deducted from the total, as can the semi-autonomous garrison of MajGen John E. Wool at Fort Monroe (9,246). This left McClellan with 104,990 men under his command. Even removing his headquarters and the army engineers (2,585 men), this still left 98,355 effectives. Now, during the week preceding the battle of Mechanicsville (26 June), the Army of the Potomac was engaged in a series of small positional battles south of the Chickahominy River. In addition it was losing men incapacitated by sickness or disease at a rate that was alarmingly put at 1,000 men a day at the time (but which has since been revealed as less than half that). It can safely be assumed that losses through action or sickness amounted

A Confederate artillery battery, in this case the Palmetto Battery (Co. I) from South Carolina. Each Confederate battery consisted of four guns, while their Union counterparts had six pieces. (Stratford Archive)

to just under 2,500 men per week. Therefore, on the eve of the campaign, McClellan had approximately 96,000 men under his command and fit for duty. During the battles that followed it became clear that the size of his army was immaterial; he was simply unable to determine where the Confederate blow would fall, and apparently reluctant to concentrate his forces to meet the enemy. Consequently an attacking army that was inferior in numbers was allowed to gain local numerical superiority over the Army of the Potomac, and to force it into retreat.

The troops themselves began the campaign with high morale. They confidently expected the army to continue its investment of Richmond, and the men knew they had a fantastic logistical train that meant they lacked for nothing; food, uniforms, ammunition, equipment and weapons. Following a reorganization of the army into smaller Corps, the Army of the Potomac was made more efficient, more maneuverable and better prepared for the coming campaign. What followed amounted to a betrayal of the confidence of this mighty army, and to the men in front of Richmond the order to retreat was met with incredulity. Put simply, McClellan created the Army of the Potomac, and then seemed reluctant to place it in harm's way. In so doing he failed his army.

THE CONFEDERATE ARMY

On 2 June 1862, General Robert E. Lee assumed command of the Confederate army outside Richmond, a loose collection of units and commands drawn together in order to defend the Confederate capital. His predecessor, General Joseph E. Johnston, had grouped his divisions into a number of ad-hoc Corps, but these formations proved something of a failure, partly due to the commanders he appointed, but largely because the army lacked the staff needed to make these large formations operate efficiently. The day after he took over the army, Lee re-named it the Army of Northern Virginia. At the time this was seen as a strange choice, as the army was hard-pressed to defend Richmond. Lee was already planning for the future, as he hoped to drive McClellan from the capital, and then take the fight north, where he had room to maneuver. In early June the effective strength of the army was just over 50,000 men. During the weeks that followed, Lee gathered whatever troops he could, including a divisional-sized force from the Military District of North Carolina, garrisons from the Atlantic coast, and most significantly "Stonewall" Jackson's Army of the Valley from the Shenandoah.

Lee remained reluctant to create Corps-sized formations. Although James Longstreet had already served as one of Johnston's ad-hoc Corps commanders, Lee used him as a Divisional commander, albeit a senior one capable of assuming command of other attached divisions as happened at Frayser's Farm during the Seven Days campaign. John Magruder commanded three divisions, but as each of these consisted of just two brigades his overall command was no bigger than that of Longstreet or A.P. Hill. However, like Longstreet, Magruder was expected to be ready to command other attached formations if required. Although this never really happened, he did assume command of some of Huger's brigades during the battles of Savage's Station and Malvern Hill. The final large formation was Jackson's Army of the Valley; a force of two divisions, those of Winder and Ewell. Lee used Jackson as a fully fledged Corps commander, and even attached Whiting's Division to Jackson's command (much to the dismay of Whiting).

Colonel James H. Childs (standing) of the 4th Pennsylvania Cavalry with his staff. His regiment was attached to Porter's V Corps. A squadron from the regiment participated in Philip Cooke's cavalry charge at Gaine's Mill. (Library of Congress)

As for the strength of the army, no detailed returns were produced immediately before the campaign began, and those that were produced earlier were confusingly given without reference to either officers or artillerymen. Several attempts have been made to determine the strength of the army, the earliest versions being produced by Confederate officers shortly after the battle. Excluding the North Carolinian reinforcements commanded by Holmes, which arrived during the campaign, but including Jackson's army, Lee's total strength at the start of the campaign has been placed at anything between 72,000 and 86,500 men. The general consensus is that he began the campaign with about 79,000 men under his command, including around 8,000 men from Jackson's Army of the Valley. Adding an estimated 6,000 men from Holmes' Division, this meant that Lee commanded around 85,000 men during the Seven Days campaign, a figure that fell far short of the 180,000–200,000 men McClellan's intelligence advisors reported. It was also numerically smaller than the Army of the Potomac although given the higher proportion of Union soldiers in non-combatant duties, the two sides began the campaign with something approaching parity in numbers.

Immediately before the campaign began, morale in the Army of Northern Virginia was generally very high. Several divisions had already experienced their first battle at Fair Oaks, and Jackson's troops considered themselves to be hardy veterans. Although the army contained raw troops, they performed well. Above all the soldiers realized that they had to win in order to save both Richmond and the Confederacy.

Lee had worked miracles in resupplying and reequipping his army since he assumed command, and the force that began the campaign was

General Porter (seated) photographed shortly after the Peninsula campaign with his headquarters staff. A staunch supporter of McClellan, he was later made a scapegoat for General Pope's humiliating defeat at Second Manassas. (University of Michigan, Anne Arbor, MI)

probably the best-equipped army the Confederates had yet fielded during the war. Supply trains had been bringing munitions and weapons to Richmond for weeks before the campaign began, while the Richmond Depot was able to furnish most of the army's logistical needs. Lee's biggest weakness was in his command structure. Lacking the Corps organization of the Army of the Potomac, he had to direct the actions of almost all his divisional commanders. At this stage in the war the divisional commanders lacked the staff they needed to effectively control their formations, and at army headquarters the situation was much worse. Many of the failures of the campaign such as the inability of Jackson to intervene effectively and the poor coordination of the army at Glendale and Malvern Hill can be blamed on poor staff work. Lee's predecessor favored a secretive style of command, and therefore failed to build up a staff that could effectively transmit orders or even maintain contact with Lee's subordinate commanders. This failure would cost Lee dearly during the coming campaign.

THE SEVEN DAYS BATTLES

THE BATTLE OF MECHANICSVILLE

General Lee's plan called for both Jackson's command and the three Richmond divisions to launch their attacks at the same time. Concerns over Jackson's ambitious timetable had already caused the Confederate attack to be delayed by a day. As dawn broke on 26 June, Lee and his subordinates firmly expected Jackson to be in position, or close enough to play his full role in the coming battle. This early in the war, poor staff work was common in both armies, and Jackson failed to provide Lee with the progress reports he needed to co-ordinate the coming battle. Worse, Lee had no firm idea where Porter's men were, or even if other Union Corps were in the vicinity of Mechanicsville. This lack of effective staff work would cost the Confederates dearly.

Porter's main line of defense lay along Beaver Dam Creek, a small marshy stream which snaked south in a lazy "S" shape through a series of ponds to reach the Chickahominy River. As Porter described it, "*The position selected on Beaver Dam Creek for our line of defense was naturally very strong. The banks of the valley were steep, and forces advancing on the adjacent plains presented their flanks as well as their front to the fire of both infantry and artillery, safe-posted behind entrenchments. The stream was over waist-deep, and bordered by swamps.*" It was a strong position, the low bluffs to the east of the creek dominating both the flatland of the creek itself, and the open ground to its front, sloping gently up to the small town of Mechanicsville

The assault of Dorsey Pender's Brigade at Mechanicsville, part of A.P. Hill's Division. The unit was halted by heavy fire from Union troops on the bluff on the far side of Beaver Dam Creek, and the unit suffered heavy casualties before it could withdraw. (Stratford Archive)

OPERATIONAL SITUATION IN THE VIRGINIA PENINSULA, 25 JUNE 1862

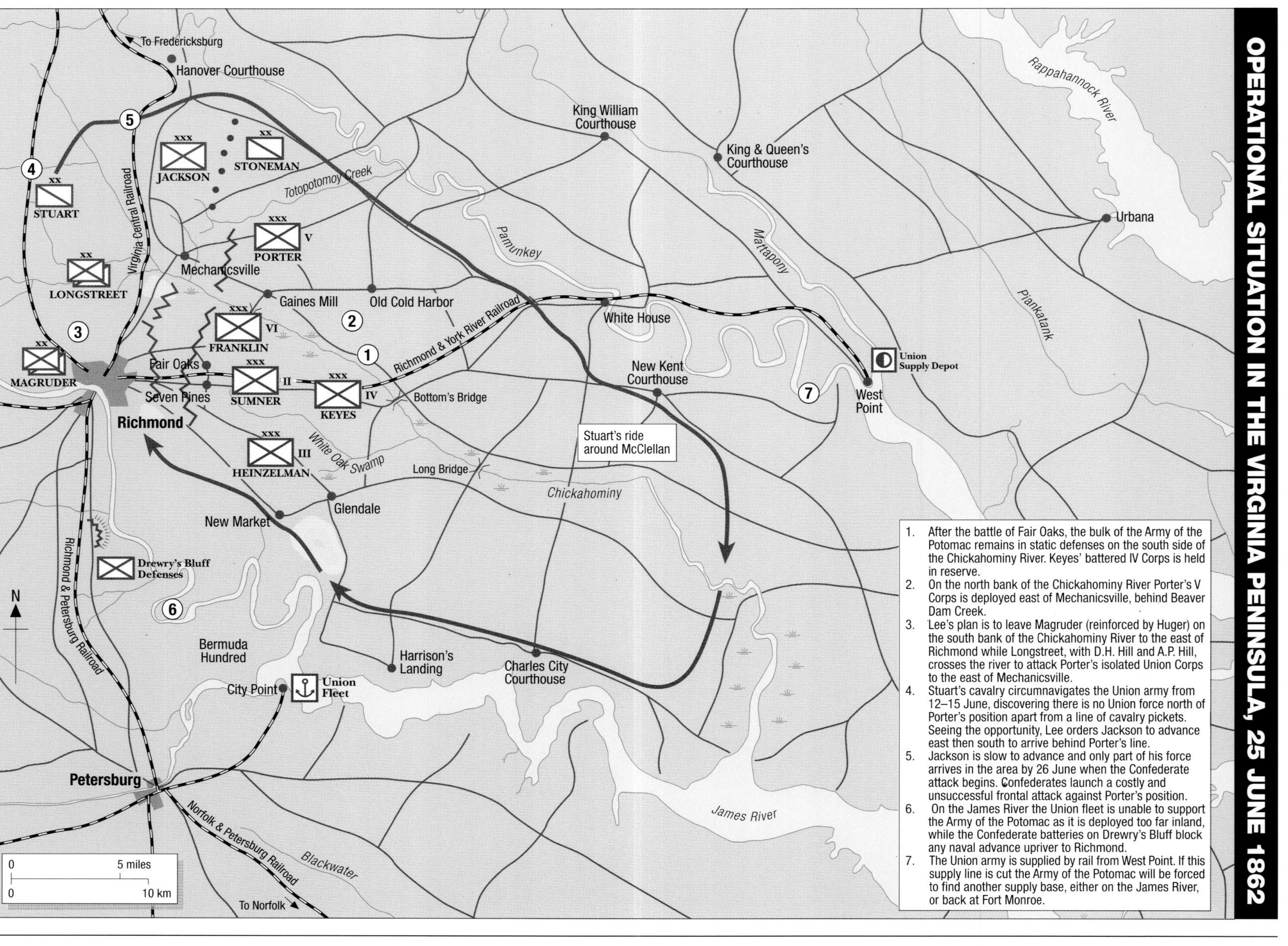

just over a mile to the west. The bends in the creek also made any attacker vulnerable to flanking fire. The Union line was held by McCall's Division, with John Reynolds' Brigade on the right (north) of Ellerson's Mill, covering the road leading east from Mechanicsville. Truman Seymour's Brigade was deployed to the left of Reynolds, while Meade's Brigade lay in reserve behind the crest of the bluffs. McCall's guns covered the western approaches to the Creek, placed to provide both frontal and flanking fire. Any attacker would be walking into a killing ground.

Porter recalled the day of the battle: *"The morning of Thursday 26th June dawned clear and bright … The formation of the ground south of the Chickahominy opposite Mechanicsville and west to Meadow Bridge largely concealed from view the forces gathered to execute an evidently well-planned attack upon my command. For some hours, on our side of the river all was quiet, except at Mechanicsville and at the two bridge crossings. At these points our small outposts were conspicuously displayed for the purpose of creating an impression of numbers and of an invitation to maintain an obstinate resistance. We aimed to win quite a heavy attack, and then, by rapid withdrawal, to incite such confidence in the enemy as to induce incautious pursuit."*

On 26 June, Major General Ambrose P. Hill (1825–65) cleared Mechanicsville of Union troops, but his division was then drawn into a rash and precipitate assault against the Union positions behind Beaver Dam Creek. (Museum of the Confederacy, Richmond, VA)

During the morning his line of outposts placed west of the creek near Mechanicsville spotted movement across the river. Worse, to the northwest scouts reported seeing vast clouds of dust in the distance, presumably marking the advance of Jackson. While Porter was prepared for a frontal attack, his right flank hung in thin air, and Jackson could turn him from his position. He wrote: *"We did not fear Lee alone. We did fear his attack combined with one by Jackson on our flank … but our fears were allayed for a day."*

Longstreet, A.P. Hill, and D.H. Hill remained inactive throughout the morning and into the early afternoon, waiting for the news that Jackson was in position. The waiting must have been even worse for Lee, as he still held fears for the safety of Richmond, should McClellan discover the city was stripped of most of its defenders. It was one of the greatest gambles of his career. For their part Magruder and Huger shared his concerns, but Magruder hoped that when the guns began to fire, the risk of a sudden attack south of the river would diminish. At noon McClellan in his headquarters at the Trent House telegraphed Washington, *"All things very quiet on this bank of the Chickahominy. I would prefer more noise."* He was about to get his way, but the cacophony would erupt on the north bank rather than the south, where the bulk of McClellan's army waited to receive a Confederate attack that never came. "Little Mac" remained convinced that what Porter was reporting was a diversion, or even the arrival of Jackson, whose approach was the subject of speculation and rumor. The notion that Lee had left the Confederate capital undefended while he massed his troops against Porter was unthinkable.

Brigadier General John F. Reynolds (1820–63) was a brigade commander in McCall's Division who played a prominent part in repulsing A.P. Hill's attack at Mechanicsville. He was captured after the battle of Gaine's Mill, but was later exchanged, only to be killed on the opening day of the battle of Gettysburg. (Stratford Archive)

The hours dragged by, and still there was no news from Jackson. Branch's Brigade, stationed northwest of Mechanicsville to serve as a link between the two forces, had heard nothing from Jackson since 9.00am, when he crossed the Richmond railroad near Ashland. Finally A.P. Hill decided he could wait no longer. *"Three o'clock having arrived and no intelligence from Jackson or Branch, I determined to cross at once, rather than hazard the failure of the whole plan by deferring it … It was never contemplated that my division alone should have sustained the shock of this battle."* He never planned to launch an impetuous assault against Porter's position behind Beaver

A Pennsylvania regiment from McCall's 3rd Division, V Corps at the battle of Mechanicsville, 26 June 1862. The Union defenders were well protected by earthworks, and had a clear field of fire over Beaver Dam Creek. (Stratford Archive)

Dam Creek. His initial objective was to clear the enemy pickets and outposts from the vicinity of the bridges, and from Mechanicsville, prior to launching a full-blown assault in conjunction with Longstreet and Jackson.

Porter described what he saw from his side of the Creek: "*About 2 o'clock, the boom of a single cannon in the direction of Mechanicsville resounded through our camps. This was the signal which had been agreed upon to announce the fact that the enemy were crossing the Chickahominy. The curtain rose, the stage was prepared for first scene of the tragedy ...*"

Lee's command post was at Chickahominy Bluff, a ridge located half a mile from the south bank of the river that overlooked Mechanicsville. Firing was heard from the Meadow Bridges to the left, and just over 30 minutes later Confederate troops were seen advancing towards Mechanicsville. "Those are A.P. Hill's men," said Lee, who masked any concern at this unexpected turn of events. He assumed Jackson had been in contact with Hill, and this advance was the prelude to a coordinated assault. Hill's men deployed and drove the gunners and skirmishers from the village, but almost immediately they came under fire from the Union guns behind Beaver Dam Creek. The time was around 3.00pm.

In Porter's words: "*About 3 o'clock the enemy under Longstreet, D.H. and A.P. Hill, in large bodies commenced rapidly to cross the Chickahominy almost simultaneously at Mechanicsville, Meadow Bridge and above, and pushed down the left bank, along the roads leading to Beaver Dam Creek. In accordance with directions previously given, the outposts watching the access to the crossings fell back after slight resistance to their already designated position on the east bank of Beaver Dam Creek, destroying the bridges as they retired.*"

A.P. Hill deployed his brigades as they arrived; the command of Charles Field facing Mechanicsville, that of Joseph R. Anderson (the owner of Richmond's Tredegar Ironworks) to the far left, while James Archer deployed between the two. Next, Dorsey Pender's Brigade (composed of the remnants of Pettigrew's and Hampton's Brigades that were mauled at Fair Oaks) deployed in line on the Old Church Road facing Ellerson's Mill.

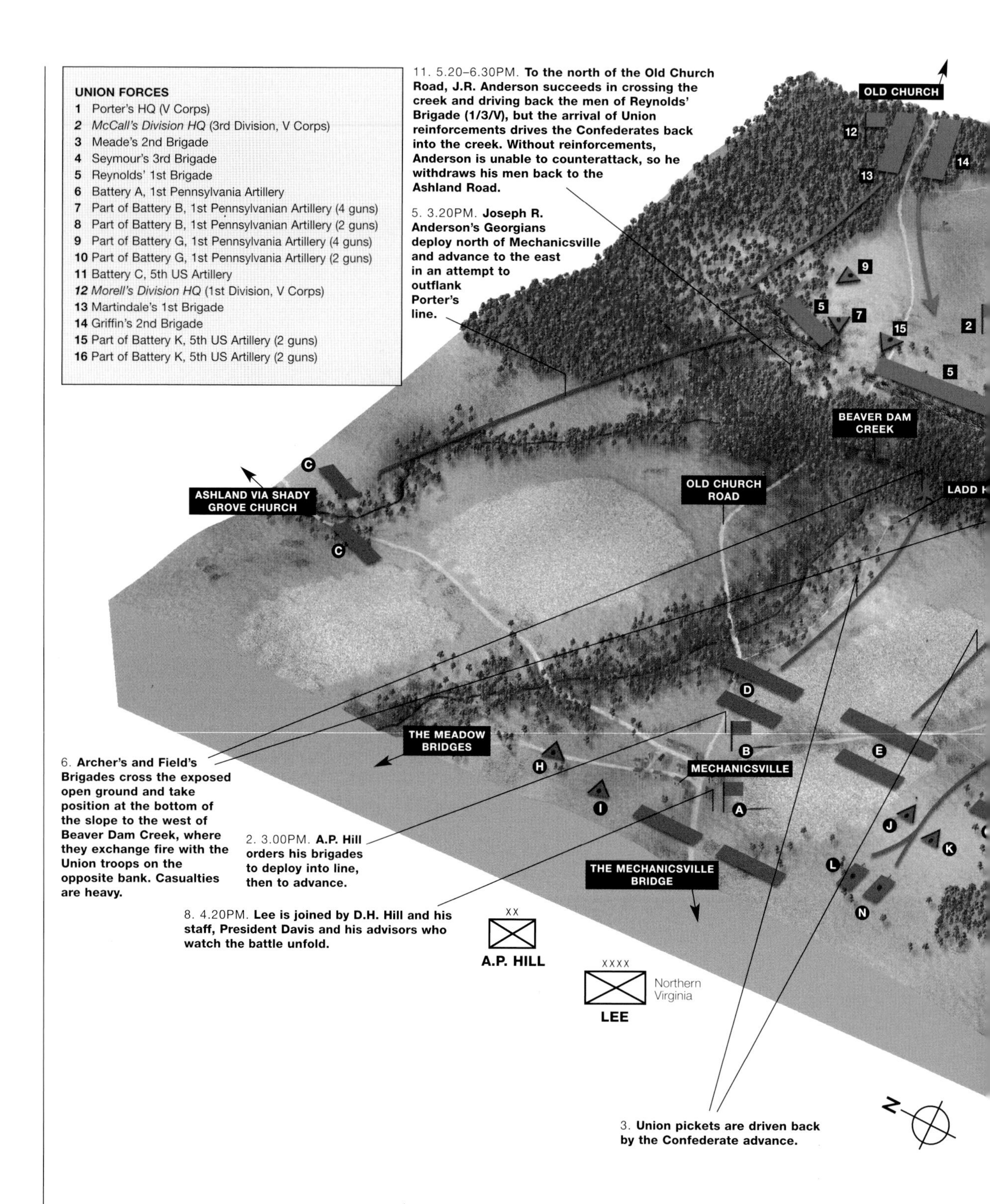

THE BATTLE OF MECHANICSVILLE

26 June 1862, viewed from the southwest. Robert E. Lee's first attack against the Union right flank was meant to be a pinning operation, allowing Thomas "Stonewall" Jackson to fall upon Porter's V Corps from the north. Jackson's failure to arrive meant that the Confederates attacking across Beaver Dam Creek were forced to make a frontal assault against a more numerous and well-entrenched enemy.

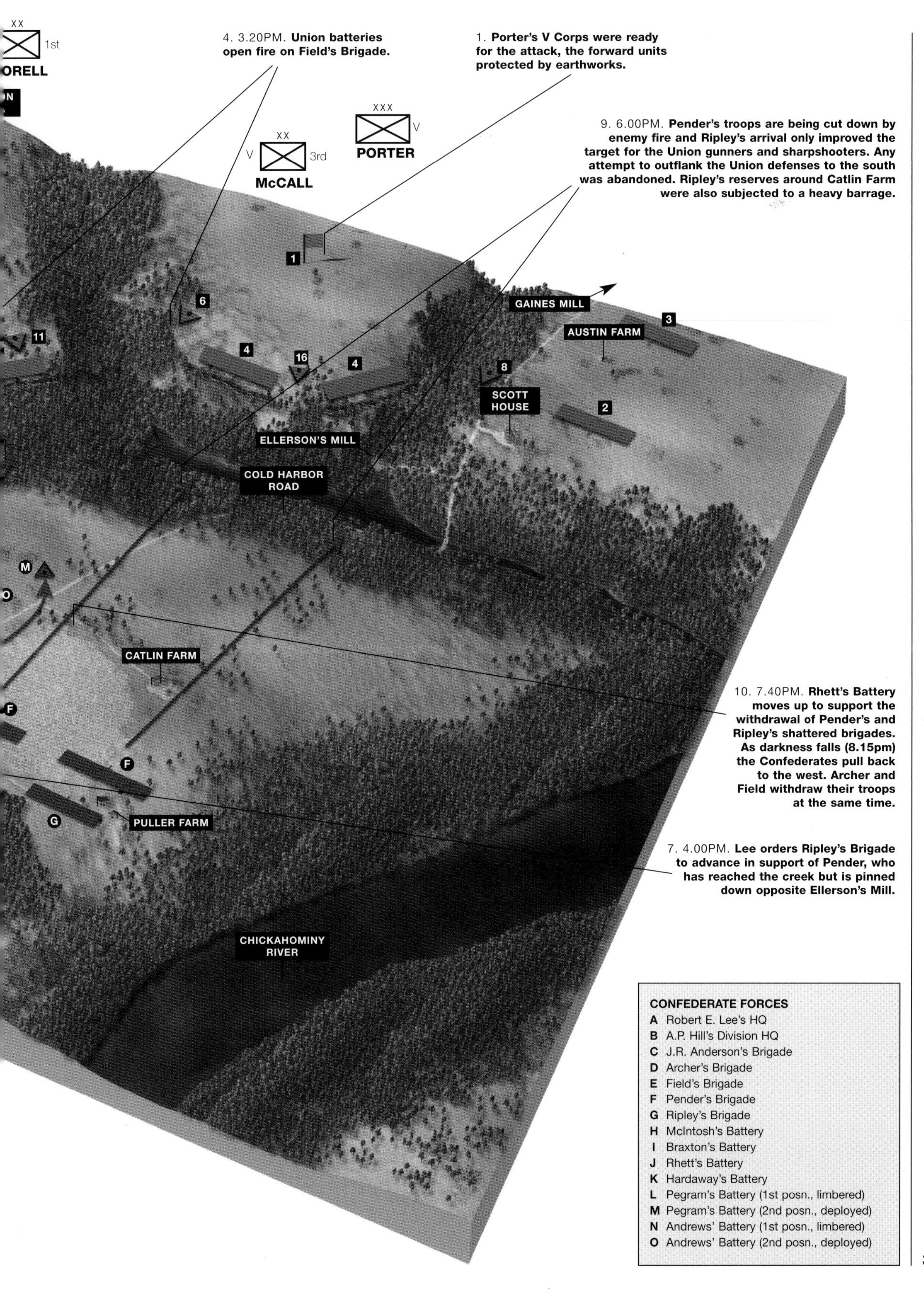

XX
1st
ORELL
4. 3.20PM. Union batteries open fire on Field's Brigade.
1. Porter's V Corps were ready for the attack, the forward units protected by earthworks.
XXX
V
PORTER
XX
V
3rd
McCALL
9. 6.00PM. Pender's troops are being cut down by enemy fire and Ripley's arrival only improved the target for the Union gunners and sharpshooters. Any attempt to outflank the Union defenses to the south was abandoned. Ripley's reserves around Catlin Farm were also subjected to a heavy barrage.
1
6
11
4
16
4
8
3
2
GAINES MILL
AUSTIN FARM
SCOTT HOUSE
ELLERSON'S MILL
COLD HARBOR ROAD
M
O
CATLIN FARM
F
F
G
PULLER FARM
10. 7.40PM. Rhett's Battery moves up to support the withdrawal of Pender's and Ripley's shattered brigades. As darkness falls (8.15pm) the Confederates pull back to the west. Archer and Field withdraw their troops at the same time.
7. 4.00PM. Lee orders Ripley's Brigade to advance in support of Pender, who has reached the creek but is pinned down opposite Ellerson's Mill.
CHICKAHOMINY RIVER
CONFEDERATE FORCES
A Robert E. Lee's HQ
B A.P. Hill's Division HQ
C J.R. Anderson's Brigade
D Archer's Brigade
E Field's Brigade
F Pender's Brigade
G Ripley's Brigade
H McIntosh's Battery
I Braxton's Battery
J Rhett's Battery
K Hardaway's Battery
L Pegram's Battery (1st posn., limbered)
M Pegram's Battery (2nd posn., deployed)
N Andrews' Battery (1st posn., limbered)
O Andrews' Battery (2nd posn., deployed)

Brigadier General William F. "Baldy" Smith (commanding 2nd Division, VI Corps) portrayed on horseback, directing his troops facing Jackson at White Oak Swamp Bridge on 30 June. Engraving of the painting by Julian Scott. (Stratford Archive)

Finally Maxcy Gregg's South Carolinians moved into position behind Pender. All this took time, and it was almost 5.00pm before A.P. Hill's Division was fully deployed around Mechanicsville, its troops under persistent fire from Porter's guns. There was still no word of Jackson, there were only three more hours of daylight left, and the troops were becoming restless. They had been expecting a battle, and seemed determined to have their way. Whether the troops began the advance themselves, or orders came from either Field or Archer is unclear, but at that moment the two brigades in the Confederate centre began to march toward the waiting Union guns. Porter described what happened next: "*After passing Mechanicsville the attacking forces were divided, a portion taking the road to the right to Ellerson's Mill, while the larger body directed their march to the left into the valley of Beaver Dam Creek, upon the road covered by Reynolds. Apparently unaware, or regardless of the great danger in their front, this force moved on with animation and confidence, as if going on parade, or engaging in a sham battle.*"

Brigadier General Porter directing his troops at Gaine's Mill. The attacking Confederates are shown approaching across the open fields to the north of the Union line, but between the two forces lay the ravine of Boatswain's Creek. Sketch by Alfred Waud. (Library of Congress)

A Union gun belonging to Heintzelman's II Corps fires over its own troops at a wave of advancing Confederate troops (probably from D.H. Hill's Division) during the battle of Malvern Hill. Sketch by Alfred Waud. (Library of Congress)

On the Confederate left, Anderson extended his line to the north, and then advanced in support of the Confederate center, his advance covered somewhat by scrub and trees. In the center, Field's Virginians and Archer's Tennessee and Georgia troops were caught in the open, crossing the deadly space in front of the Union guns. Porter recalled: "*Suddenly, when halfway down the bank of the valley, our men opened up in rapid volleys of artillery and infantry, which strewed the road and hillside with hundreds of dead and wounded, and drove the main body of the survivors back in rapid flight to and beyond Mechanicsville.*"

This was not strictly accurate, as while Field's men managed to withdraw, many of Archer's troops went to ground in hollows, or charged forward to the tree line in front of the Creek. The Union troops fired as if on exercise, and the attack ground to a halt in a hail of shot. According to Porter, *"Some of Reynolds' ammunition was exhausted, and two regiments were relieved by the 4th Michigan and 14th New York of Griffin's Brigade."* Porter had troops to spare. Anderson had a little more success, managing to cross the creek. As Porter put it, "*On the extreme right a small force of the enemy secured a foothold on the east bank, but it did no harm.*" Unsupported, Anderson could achieve very little.

Together with other Richmond residents, Governor John Letcher watched the battle unfold from the roof of his mansion. Also watching from Richmond, Southern diarist Judith McGuire recalled that, "*the commanding hills from the President's house to the Almshouse were covered, like a vast amphitheatre, with men women and children witnessing the grand display of fireworks – beautiful – yet awful, and sending death amid those whom our hearts hold so dear ... the brilliant light of bombs bursting in the air and passing to the ground, the innumerable lesser lights emitted by thousands and thousands of muskets, together with the roar of artillery and the rattling of small arms, constituted a scene terrifically grand and imposing.*

The next Confederate mistake was to reinforce failure. Branch's Brigade arrived at Mechanicsville, after having failed to link up with Jackson. It formed a reserve, while D.H. Hill sent Ripley's North Carolina Brigade across the Mechanicsville Bridge to support A.P. Hill. These fresh troops deployed on the Confederate right, and their arrival led to a fresh

CS

THE ATTACK OF PENDER'S BRIGADE AT MECHANICSVILLE, 26 JUNE 1862 (pages 34-35)

Beaver Dam Creek (1) **Creek represented a formidable obstacle to the Confederate attackers. Although the slow-moving creek was only a few yards wide and less than four feet deep in most places, a gently rising area of open but boggy ground lay beyond it, leading to the foot of a low bluff. Immediately to the south, beyond Ellerson's Mill (out of sight some 400 yards to the right of the scene, on the far bank of the creek), a narrow millpond some 1,200 yards long presented an impassable barrier. All approaches were covered by Union fire. A line of rifle pits and hastily-improvised earthworks stretched along the foot of the bluff** (2)**, where detached companies of Union defenders were able to pour point-blank fire into the Confederates who were trapped along the west bank of the Creek. The section of the Union line shown here was defended by men from the 10th Pennsylvania Reserves, part of Brigadier General Truman Seymour's 3rd Brigade of Brigadier General McCall's 3rd Division, part of V Corps. Behind them, on the crest of the hill the main line of defense ran along the crest of the bluff** (3)**, extending from a point a half-mile north of the ford where the Old Church Road crossed Beaver Dam Creek. It ended a half-mile south of this scene, a quarter of a mile south of Ellerson's Mill. In the portion of the Union line shown in this view, the main line was held by the 1st Pennsylvania Volunteers, part of Brigadier General John F. Reynolds' 1st Brigade of McCall1s Division, supported by the six guns of C Battery, 5th US Artillery, plus two more guns from Battery G, 1st Pennsylvania Light Artillery, deployed on the right flank of the 1st Pennsylvania Volunteers. The Confederate formations who charged this portion of the Union line were the brigades of Brigadier Generals Charles W. Field and William D. Pender, a Virginian and a North Carolinian formation respectively. The Confederate troops in this scene are the intermingled regiments of the 16th and 22nd North Carolina Volunteers, who formed the left flank of Pender's Brigade during the attack. They suffered heavy casualties from the Union guns on the ridge as they crossed the 1,000 yards of open ground between their starting positions just south of Mechanicsville and the Creek. Finding themselves unable to cross without being cut down, the survivors sheltered along the line of the creek** (4)**, firing back as best they could. Further to the north** (5) **Field's Brigade and the troops of Brigadier General James J. Archer1s Brigade were also halted by enemy fire before they could cross the creek. Any further advance proved impossible. Worse, the troops were unable to retire back across the open fields behind them without exposing themselves again to the Union guns mounted on the top of the bluff east of the creek. At least on the creek bed they were relatively safe from artillery fire, although they were still vulnerable to small-arms fire from the troops facing them. Casualties continued to mount** (6)**, until as darkness fell the pinned Confederates were able to withdraw back across the fields behind them to safety. (Stephen Walsh)**

Union artillery at the battle of Gaine's Mill. Porter lost over 30 guns during the closing moments of the battle. (Stratford Archive)

assault, the Carolinians supported on their left by Pender's Brigade. The two Confederate brigades headed toward Ellerson's Mill. Porter described the outcome of the assault: "*The forces which were directed against Seymour at Ellerson's Mill made little progress. Seymour's direct and Reynolds' flank fire soon arrested them and drove them to shelter, suffering even more disastrously than those who had attacked Reynolds. Late in the afternoon, greatly strengthened, they renewed the attack with spirit and energy, some reaching the borders of the stream, but only to be repulsed with terrible slaughter, which warned them not to attempt a renewal of the fight.*"

The crowds watching from Richmond had a grandstand view of a costly debacle. Edward Pollard recalled that; "*Barns, houses, and stacks of hay and straw were in a blaze; and by their light our men were plainly visible rushing across the open spaces through infernal showers of grape.*" Other observers were less willing to witness the slaughter. Mrs Roger A. Prior refused to watch, as her husband was a Brigadier in Lee's army. "*I shut myself in my darkened room,*" she wrote. "*At twilight I had a note from Governor Letcher ... inviting me to come to the governor's mansion. From the roof one might see the flash of musket and artillery. No! ... I preferred to wait alone in my room.*" Her husband survived the battle unscathed, but many were not so lucky. As darkness fell the dead and dying littered the mile of open ground between Mechanicsville and the Creek. Porter recalled how: "*Little depressions in the ground shielded many from our fire, until, when night came, they all fell back beyond the range of our guns. Night brought an end to the contest.*"

Nearly 1,500 Confederate soldiers fell at Mechanicsville, while Porter lost around 360 men killed or wounded. Lee's first attack of the campaign was a costly failure, and Jackson never arrived to save the day. Daniel H. Hill summed up the battle several years later when he wrote: "*We were lavish of blood in those days, and it was thought to be a great thing to charge a battery of artillery or an earthwork lined with infantry.*" In the Union camp Surgeon Stevens wrote: "*Men who had, by constant hardships and by continually looking on death, almost forgotten the feelings of joy now broke out in loud shouts of gladness; and for the first time in many weeks the bands played those heart-stirring national airs which in times past have been wont to fill the heart of the soldiers with enthusiasm ... A renewal of the attack might be expected at any moment. Still, the men of the whole of the left wing were exulting in the grand hope that in the morning we were to march into Richmond almost without*

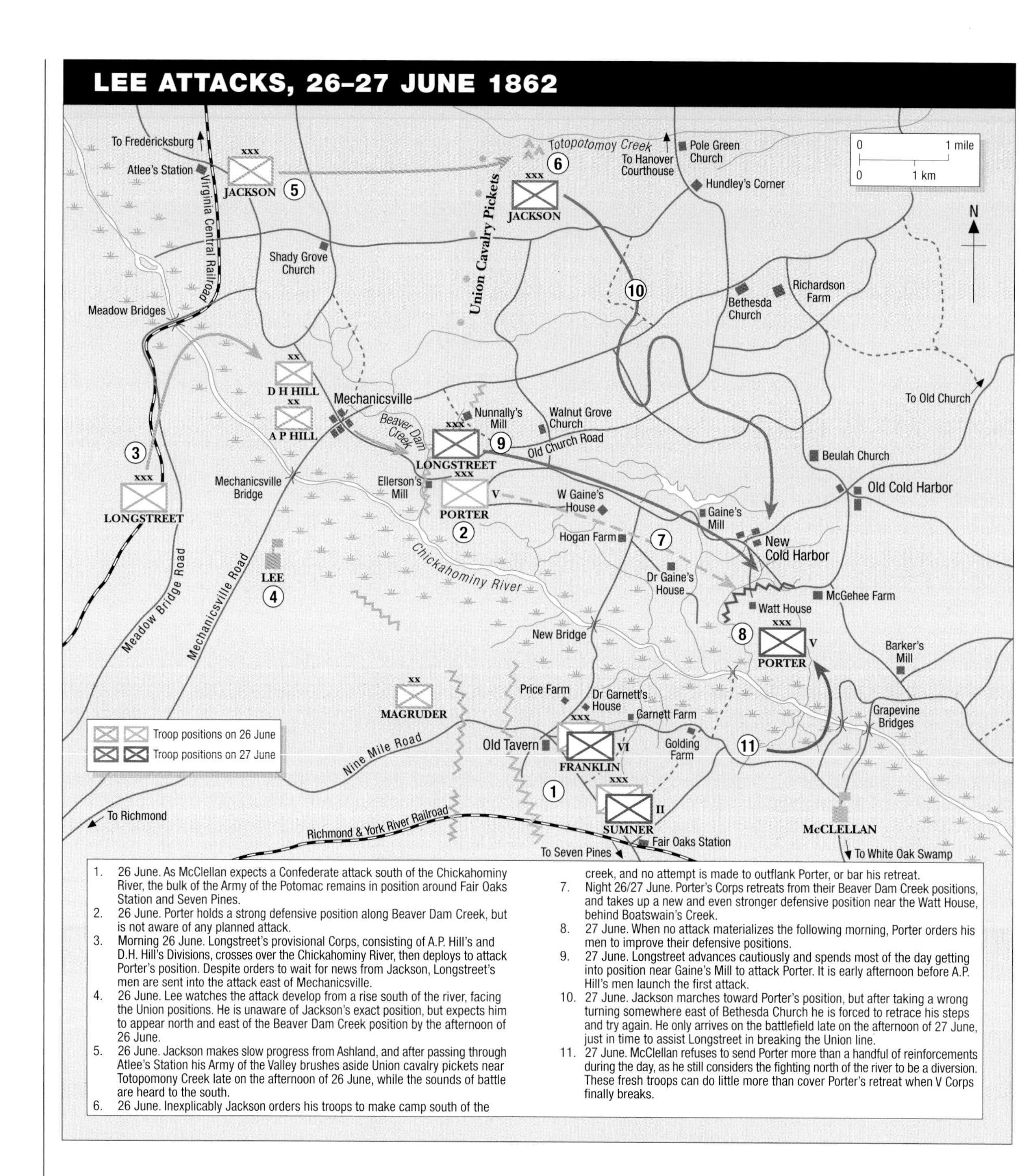

opposition … The prize which they had so often been promised seemed almost within the grasp." Clearly the surgeon had a better grasp of strategy than his commanding officer.

At 9.00pm McClellan wired Secretary of War Stanton from the Trent House with the news: "*Victory of today complete and against great odds. I almost begin to think we are invincible.*" However, that night his old doubts reappeared. Unlike Surgeon Stevens and his companions in the front line, McClellan was unable to see the opportunity Lee's attack had presented. He still thought Lee outnumbered him on both sides of the river. Worse,

An artillery battery of McCall's Division firing on the attacking Confederates of A.P. Hill's Division at Mechanicsville. Some 24 guns were sited on the bluff overlooking Beaver Dam Creek. Sketch by Alfred Waud. (Library of Congress)

he was aware that Jackson was now encamped a few miles northeast of Mechanicsville, and thereby threatened Porter's flank. If the battle resumed in the morning, Porter would find himself cut off, and on the wrong side of the river. McClellan was already beginning the process of moving his supply base from the York to the James River. A more aggressive commander might decide that this being the case, he could afford to temporarily lose his lines of communication, and instead defend with Porter, while the rest of his army drove forward on Richmond, attacking where Lee was weakest. Instead he did nothing apart from give Porter orders to pull back. At 3.00am, orders arrived at V Corps headquarters for an orderly withdrawal from Beaver Dam Creek to Gaine's Mill, where a new defensive position would be established behind Boatswain's Creek, protecting the Grapevine Bridge crossing of the Chickahominy. Given the presence of Jackson nobody can fault McClellan for ordering this withdrawal, although he never even considered letting Porter remain in

Men of the 4th Texas Regiment (part of John B. Hood's Brigade) storming the Union guns on top of the bluff at Gaine's Mill. Their breakthrough was the turning point of the battle. Sketch by Alfred Waud. (Library of Congress)

position, and sending troops to protect his northern flank. Instead he ordered the first withdrawal of the Seven Days, while the rest of his army did nothing. This pattern of inactivity and withdrawal would be repeated all the way to the James River.

THE BATTLE OF GAINE'S MILL

As dawn broke A.P. Hill sent patrols forward to probe the Union line, but apart from a few skirmishers he found the Union positions deserted.

Porter described these events in his report: "*Before sunrise on the 27th, the troops were withdrawn from Beaver Dam Creek and sent to their new positions east of Powhite Creek, destroying the bridges across it after them. Some batteries and infantry skirmishers, left as a ruse at Beaver Dam Creek, by their fire so fully absorbed the attention of the foe that our purpose suddenly and rapidly to abandon our entrenchments seemed unsuspected. But when they discovered our withdrawal their infantry pressed forward in small detachments, the main body and the artillery being delayed to rebuild the bridges.*"

By noon, A.P. Hill's men were marching east in pursuit of Porter, and the rest of the army followed them. Jackson made slow progress from Hundley's Corner, but he advanced south toward Walnut Grove Church, where he encountered his old classmate Ambrose Hill. The two generals exchanged pleasantries for a few minutes, and then Robert E. Lee arrived with his staff. Hill resumed his advance, while Lee and Jackson met in the grove beside the church. Nobody knows exactly what transpired, but immediately afterwards Jackson rode off to lead his troops toward Cold Harbor. Lee and his generals expected to find the Union army behind Powhite Creek (pronounced "pow-height"), and also suspected that by this stage McClellan had moved some of his other Corps up to support Porter. Equally critical was to advance as far as Dr. Gaine's House on the Telegraph Road, where another road ran south to the New Bridge over the Chickahominy River. This would provide a link with Magruder, and meant that if McClellan attacked south of the river, Lee could now move to support his isolated commanders in front of Richmond.

McClellan had no such intention. At 10.00am on the morning of 27 June he wired Secretary of War Stanton to report that Porter's "change of position" had been *"beautifully executed under a sharp fire, with little loss. The troops on the other side* [i.e. the north bank of the Chickahominy River] *are now well in hand, and the whole army so concentrated that it can take advantage of the first mistake made by the enemy."* He had been presented with a superb opportunity to storm Richmond. Instead, McClellan left his troops in situ south of the river, and left Porter isolated north of the Chickahominy River. Worse, he was becoming obsessed with the threat to his supply lines.

Porter assumed his role was to hold on in his position near Gaine's Mill until reinforcements arrived. After all, his men were the only sizeable Union detachment capable of protecting the Union lines of supply. He was unaware that McClellan had already planned to abandon his supply base at White House, and Porter's VI Corps was buying time for the supply wagons to make the trip from their old base to their new position at Harrison's Landing, on the James River. As this new base lacked any railroad connection leading to Richmond, the decision to abandon the

Major General Daniel H. Hill (1821–89) was one of Lee's most gifted divisional commanders, although he developed a reputation for recklessness as well as courage. Later in the war his criticism of both Robert E. Lee and Braxton Bragg earned him the disapproval of President Davis. (Valentine Museum, Richmond, VA).

Brigadier General John Bell Hood (1831–79) distinguished himself at Gaine's Mill when the charge of his brigade broke the Union line. Although closely associated with Texas, Hood was actually born in Owingsville, Kentucky. (Stratford Archive)

Franklin's VI Corps retreating past the burning supply dump at Savage's Station during the evening of 29 June. The unit in the foreground can be identified as the 16th New York by the distinctive straw boaters worn by the soldiers. Sketch by Alfred Waud. (Library of Congress)

White House was tantamount to an admission of defeat. With his engineer's mind, McClellan assumed that his siege train would play a crucial role in the capture of Richmond. As it could only be moved forward by rail or river, and there was no facilities to advance the siege guns from Harrison's Landing, McClellan was planning to retreat from the Confederate capital rather than advance toward it. Brigadier General Silas Casey, who commanded the garrison at the White House, was ordered to embark whatever stores he could, and send the rest by wagon to the new base. This would all take time, and in the meantime, Porter was ordered to hold his ground. If he broke, the road from White House to Harrison's Landing could be cut, and the army would lose its supplies.

The loyal Porter wrote: I *"Though in a desperate situation, I was not without strong hope of some timely assistance from the main body of the army, with which I might repulse the attack and so cripple our opponents as to make the capture of Richmond by the main body of the army, under McClellan, the result ... I felt that the life or death of the Army depended on our conduct in this contest ... and that on the issue of that contest depended an early peace or a prolonged, devastating war."*

McClellan was unwilling to take advantage of Porter's sacrifice to storm Richmond. The rest of the army was as surprised as Porter that no attack was launched, and Franklin's troops watched Porter's men retreat north of the river, pursued by the Confederate army. McClellan was still concerned that the Confederates would attack south of the river, and ordered his troops there to stand in readiness to receive an attack. Chaplain Stuart reported that the enemy was so close that conversations from the Confederate lines could be heard with ease. This, and the increased instance of orders being shouted, drums rolling and bugle calls suggested an attack might still take place. Instead it was "Prince John" Magruder, the expert in the art of battlefield deception, up to his old tricks. It was all a ruse in the style of the one he pulled off so successfully outside Yorktown, and once again, McClellan took the bait. The real battle would take place north of the river, where Porter's V Corps stood isolated, with its back to the river.

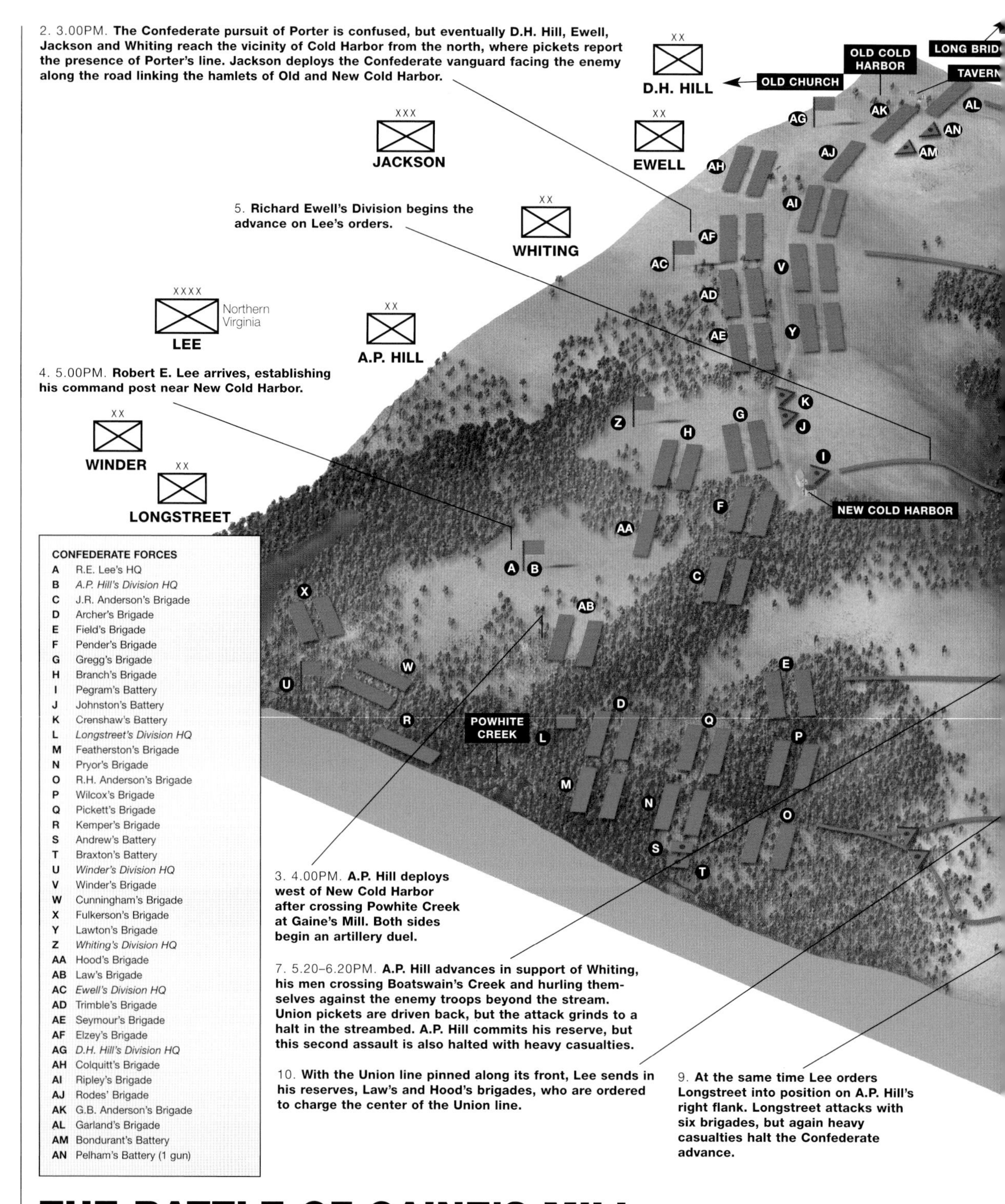

THE BATTLE OF GAINE'S MILL

27 June 1862, viewed from the southwest. After Mechanicsville, Porter withdrew behind Boatswain's Creek, a superb defensive position protecting the crossings over the Chickahominy River. Reinforced by "Stonewall" Jackson, Lee launched a series of costly frontal attacks against the Union position, forcing Porter to fight all along his line. Victory would go to the commander who displayed the greatest will to win, regardless of the cost.

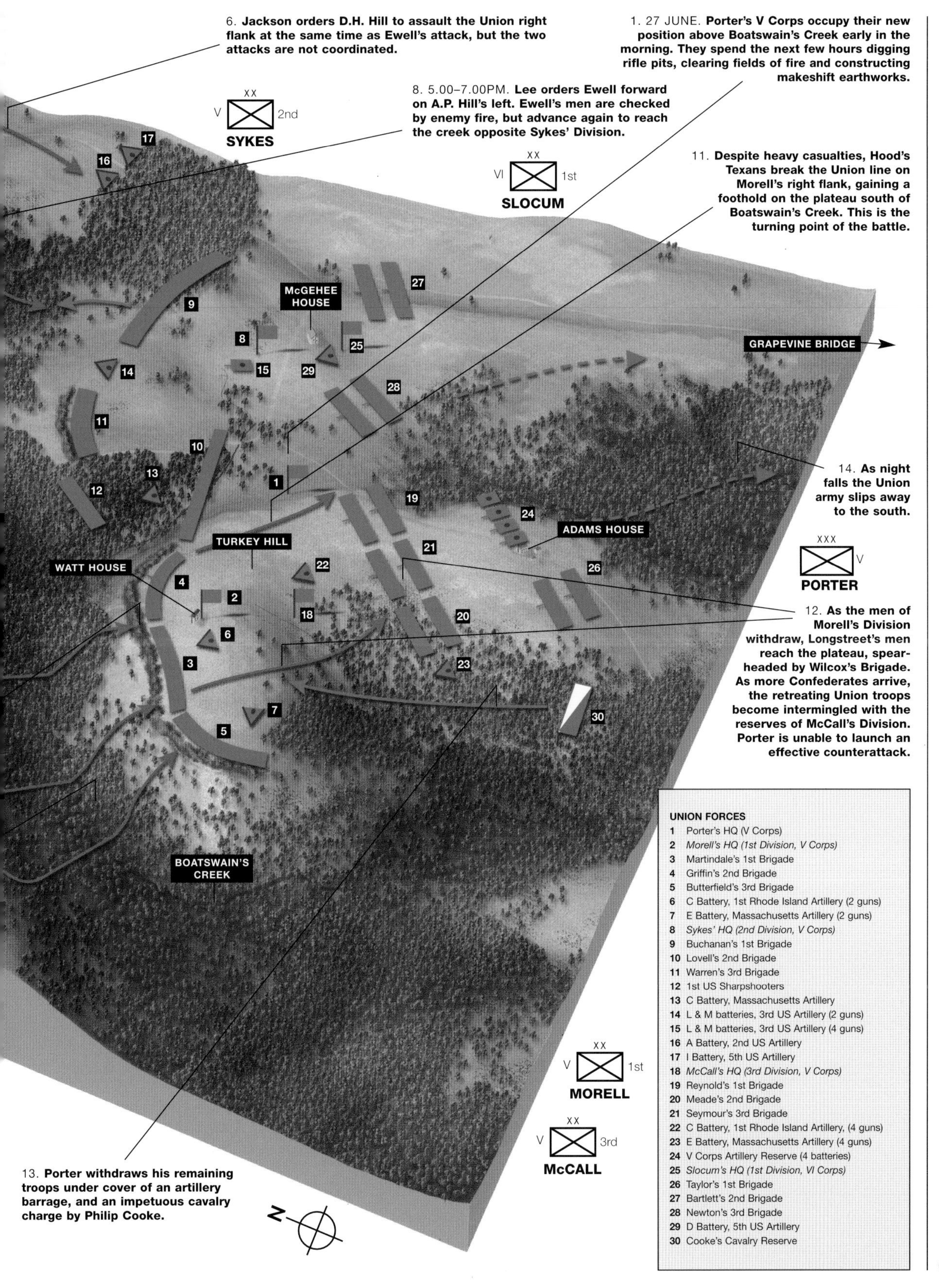

6. Jackson orders D.H. Hill to assault the Union right flank at the same time as Ewell's attack, but the two attacks are not coordinated.
1. 27 JUNE. Porter's V Corps occupy their new position above Boatswain's Creek early in the morning. They spend the next few hours digging rifle pits, clearing fields of fire and constructing makeshift earthworks.
8. 5.00–7.00PM. Lee orders Ewell forward on A.P. Hill's left. Ewell's men are checked by enemy fire, but advance again to reach the creek opposite Sykes' Division.
XX
V
2nd
SYKES
XX
VI
1st
SLOCUM
11. Despite heavy casualties, Hood's Texans break the Union line on Morell's right flank, gaining a foothold on the plateau south of Boatswain's Creek. This is the turning point of the battle.
McGEHEE HOUSE
GRAPEVINE BRIDGE
14. As night falls the Union army slips away to the south.
TURKEY HILL
ADAMS HOUSE
WATT HOUSE
XXX
V
PORTER
12. As the men of Morell's Division withdraw, Longstreet's men reach the plateau, spear-headed by Wilcox's Brigade. As more Confederates arrive, the retreating Union troops become intermingled with the reserves of McCall's Division. Porter is unable to launch an effective counterattack.
BOATSWAIN'S CREEK
XX
V
1st
MORELL
XX
V
3rd
McCALL
13. Porter withdraws his remaining troops under cover of an artillery barrage, and an impetuous cavalry charge by Philip Cooke.
N
UNION FORCES
1 Porter's HQ (V Corps)
2 Morell's HQ (1st Division, V Corps)
3 Martindale's 1st Brigade
4 Griffin's 2nd Brigade
5 Butterfield's 3rd Brigade
6 C Battery, 1st Rhode Island Artillery (2 guns)
7 E Battery, Massachusetts Artillery (2 guns)
8 Sykes' HQ (2nd Division, V Corps)
9 Buchanan's 1st Brigade
10 Lovell's 2nd Brigade
11 Warren's 3rd Brigade
12 1st US Sharpshooters
13 C Battery, Massachusetts Artillery
14 L & M batteries, 3rd US Artillery (2 guns)
15 L & M batteries, 3rd US Artillery (4 guns)
16 A Battery, 2nd US Artillery
17 I Battery, 5th US Artillery
18 McCall's HQ (3rd Division, V Corps)
19 Reynold's 1st Brigade
20 Meade's 2nd Brigade
21 Seymour's 3rd Brigade
22 C Battery, 1st Rhode Island Artillery, (4 guns)
23 E Battery, Massachusetts Artillery (4 guns)
24 V Corps Artillery Reserve (4 batteries)
25 Slocum's HQ (1st Division, VI Corps)
26 Taylor's 1st Brigade
27 Bartlett's 2nd Brigade
28 Newton's 3rd Brigade
29 D Battery, 5th US Artillery
30 Cooke's Cavalry Reserve

Soldiers from Brigadier General Philip Kearny's 3rd Division, III Corps firing at the advancing Confederates of Longstreet's Division during the battle of Frayser's Farm, 30 June. They held a line just south of the Charles City Road, northwest of the Glendale crossroads. Sketch by Alfred Waud. (Library of Congress)

Noon passed as A.P. Hill's troops crossed Powhite Creek at Gaine's Mill and began deploying in the open fields in front of New Cold Harbor facing Porter's line, which they discovered lay on the southern side of Boatswain's Creek. A.P. Hill's Division was the first on the field, having encamped around Mechanicsville the night before. D.H. Hill took a more roundabout route, using the Old Church Road as a line of advance, then cutting down towards the right of the Union line at Old Cold Harbor. Longstreet followed the road that ran parallel to the north bank of the Chickahominy River, reaching Powhite Creek east of Dr Gaine's House. As for Jackson, he headed east from Walnut Grove Church, then turned south on the road running from Bethesda Church to New Cold Harbor. After a mile or so he realized he was on the wrong road, as Lee had asked him to deploy to the east of A.P. Hill, not behind him. Consequently Jackson retraced his steps and then followed the

The hamlet of Mechanicsville was little more than a collection of small wooden cabins, with one more substantial house in the center of the village. A.P. Hill's Division cleared Union skirmishers from its buildings before embarking on their assault against Porter's line at Beaver Dam Creek on 26 June. (Stratford Archive)

This engraving based on the Alfred Waud sketch of the retreat of VI Corps through Savage's Station has been expanded to show, in the foreground, guns from Sumner's II Corps left behind to hold the line. (Stratford Archive)

road that curved round to Old Cold Harbor, marching behind D.H. Hill's column.

Lee established his headquarters in a farmhouse near the battlefield, and waited for his generals to move into position. Around 12.30pm the battle began as A.P. Hill sent forward his skirmish lines, driving the Union picket lines back toward Boatswain's Creek. Lieutenant Caldwell from South Carolina described the action: "*We moved forward and drove a strong skirmish* [line] *from a pine thicket just beyond the Mill, at the double quick … We shot down several of the enemy as they retreated across the open field.*" This allowed A.P. Hill to deploy his division facing the center of Porter's line, but it was 2.00pm before he launched the first attack of the day. Porter was watching the Confederate advance: *"Dashing across the intervening plain, floundering in the swamps, and struggling against the tangled brushwood, brigade after brigade seemed almost to melt away before the concentrated fire of our artillery and infantry; yet others pressed on, followed by supports as dashing and brave as their predecessors, despite the heavy losses and the disheartening effect of having to clamber over many of their disabled and dead, and to meet their surviving comrades rushing back in great disorder from the deadly contest."* It was a slaughter. These were the men who experienced their baptism of fire the day before when they crossed the deadly ground at Mechanicsville. At Gaine's Mill they did it again, and within an hour the brigades of A.P. Hill's command were broken. The assault had been concentrated against the sector of the Union line held by Morell's Division (1st Division, V Corps). Most Confederates never even made it to the creek, but the North Carolinians of Lawrence Branch and Dorsey Pender's Brigades managed to reach the slope above the Creek before retiring, broken by the intense fire. Maxcy Gregg's South Carolina brigade actually managed to cross the Creek on Morell's right, only to run into the concentrated fire of the US Regulars from Lovell's Brigade, and the 5th New York Zouaves, one of the two regiments in Warren's Brigade. Gregg's attack was halted. Private John Urban of McCall's Division recalled the fighting: *"One of the fiercest conflicts that occurred … was fought by Colonel Duryea's regiment of Zouaves* [5th New York] *and a large force of rebels …* [who] *charged with frantic yells … The Zouaves poured into their ranks a deadly fire, and then, with a wild shout charged* [with] *bayonets … Then ensued a conflict as terrible as human beings*

The destruction of the White House, home of Rooney Lee, by the men of Brigadier-General Silas Casey's garrison following McClellan's order to abandon his supply base at White House Landing. (Library of Congress)

can make it ... Neither side appeared to think of loading their muskets, but depended entirely on the bayonet ... by the time we reached the ground the gallant fellows had beaten the rebels back into the woods and out of sight. They had, however, paid dearly for their victory, as about 300 ... lay dead or terribly wounded on the field". Gregg's South Carolinians lost 815 men that day, more than any other brigade on the field.

Porter later wrote: *"For nearly two hours the battle raged ... the fierce firing artillery and infantry, the crash of the shot, the bursting of shells, and whizzing of bullets, heard above the roar of artillery ... The regiments quickly replenished or exhausted ammunition by borrowing from the more badly supplied and generous companions. Some withdrew, temporarily, for ammunition, and fresh regiments took a place ready to repulse ... the desperate enemy."*

Lee was concerned that Porter might launch a counterattack against A.P. Hill's broken troops, but the arrival of Richard Ewell's Division (part of Jackson's Command) at New Cold Harbor ended the risk. Lee rode over to the left and met Jackson riding east. Lee spoke: *"Ah, General, I am very glad to see you. I had hoped to have been with you before."* Lee ordered Jackson to send Ewell into the attack. The first of Ewell's brigades to reach the battlefield was the Louisiana formation of Isaac Seymour. It advanced toward the area where Gregg's Brigade had crossed, then hurled itself across the Creek, spearheaded by the Louisiana Tigers. The attack was checked by intense fire, and when Seymour fell the Louisiana troops began to retire. Their place was taken by Isaac Trimble's men, who faltered in the Creek, then stood their ground and traded point-blank volleys with the US Regulars from Sykes' Division (2nd Div., V Corps). The attack ended when Porter pushed his reserves (McCall's 3rd Division) into the line.

It was at this point that Longstreet arrived on A.P. Hill's right, the western end of the field. Lee ordered him to make an attack as a diversion, to relieve pressure on A.P. Hill and Ewell. His attack was spearheaded by George Pickett's Virginia Brigade, which was soon driven back by intense fire as they reached the creek. The rest of Longstreet's brigades made no more headway. Then a Union counterattack

Major General Richard S. Ewell (1817–72), Jackson's trusted lieutenant who led a vigorous assault against the Union lines at Gaine's Mill on 27 June. Painting by J.P. Walker (Virginia Historical Society, Richmond, VA)

Brigadier General Silas Casey (1807–82) commanded the division that bore the brunt of the Confederate assault at Fair Oaks (31 May), and was then reassigned to command the garrison at White House Landing. (National Archives)

appeared, launched by units from Slocum's 1st Division of VI Corps, which had crossed the river to support Porter, and arrived in time to drive Longstreet's men back beyond the Creek. One man in four from Longstreet's Division was either killed or wounded that afternoon. Confederate Cavalryman John E. Cooke later wrote: *"Such was the state of affairs on the field about five in the evening. The Federals troops had repulsed every assault, and the descending sun threatened to set upon a day memorable in the annals of the South for bloody and disastrous defeat."*

Further reinforcements began to arrive. Around 4.00pm D.H. Hill's men began to appear at Old Cold Harbor, and less than an hour later William Whiting's men arrived, his two brigades ordered into the line in place of A.P. Hill's men. Charles Winder's Division also arrived, and formed up behind the remnants of Ewell's brigades. The battle was entering a second phase, and Lee would have one last throw of the dice. A natural lull in the fighting occurred, but by 6.45pm Lee was ready to launch a final assault. Lieutenant Caldwell noted that, *"The great Lee seemed to be ubiquitous, here sending in a fresh brigade, here dispatching couriers to various quarters of the field, here rallying and reassuring a disordered regiment, constantly in motion but always sublimely brave and calm."* He realized the importance of the moment. On the left of the Confederate line D.H. Hill's five brigades advanced in line, trying to hook round the right flank of Sykes' Division. Keeping formation was practically impossible as these troops entered the wooded undergrowth south of Old Cold Harbor. They emerged from the woods in front of the McGehee House, where Robert Buchanan's Brigade[2], was deployed in line, supported by a portion of Slocum's Division. D.H. Hill dressed his ranks and ordered an advance across the 400 yards of deadly space, and they managed to maintain the momentum despite heavy casualties, forcing the regulars of Sykes' Division to give ground. Meanwhile Winder launched his own attack against Sykes' center, and here too the Confederates managed to make progress, gaining a foothold across the Creek. On the Confederate right, Longstreet launched his men in another assault, and he advanced into the teeth of the fire from his front, while taking enfilading artillery fire from Union batteries across the Chickahominy River, a mile to the south. Although the Alabama troops of Cadmus Wilcox's Brigade managed to work their way up the slope beyond the Creek, they were halted when their brigade commander was killed. Porter's troops were under pressure all along the line, but it looked as if they might be able to hold. Then Whiting's two brigades entered the fray. They advanced on Longstreet's left, holding their fire until they scrambled down the bank into the creek. At that point the Union defenders were in three lines – one at the foot of the slope, one in a line of rifle pits halfway up, and a final line at the crest. The men of John Bell Hood's and Evander McIver Law's brigades fired a devastating volley at point-blank range, then charged with a Rebel Yell that *"sounded like forty thousand wildcats."* This was more than enough for Morell's men who fled up the hill, taking the second line with them as they fled. Both Confederate brigades fired into the mass of routing men then scrambled after them. It was the 4th Texas from Hood's Brigade who reached the crest first, vaulting the breastworks to

2 1st Brigade, 2nd Division, V Corps.

The Chickahominy River was a wide, marshy area of river and wetland that could only be crossed by bridge. The boggy ground also meant that approach ramps had to be constructed to permit the use of the bridges by McClellan's guns and wagons. This photograph shows the southern approach to Grapevine Bridge. (Library of Congress)

gain a foothold on the plateau in front of the Watts House. Hood's Brigade suffered heavily that day; the 4th Texas alone lost 256 men killed or wounded out of the 530 men who had marched behind the flag that morning. However, their assault was the turning point of the battle, and helped turn defeat into victory.

The Union line began to cave in, allowing the rest of the attackers to gain the crest. Porter had already committed his reserves (Slocum and McCall's Divisions), so he had no body of fresh troops to throw into the fight. The Union retreat spread along the line, and within minutes the retreat had become general. The Confederates followed up, over-running artillery pieces after shooting the horses, and capturing isolated pockets of Union troops who had failed to retreat in time.

George Cook made a futile attempt to stem the tide by launching a mounted charge against the advancing Confederates between the

The battle of Savage's Station, showing Brigadier General Sumner and his staff in the middle foreground, and the burning railroad yard on the right of the scene. Sketch by Arthur Lumley. (Library of Congress)

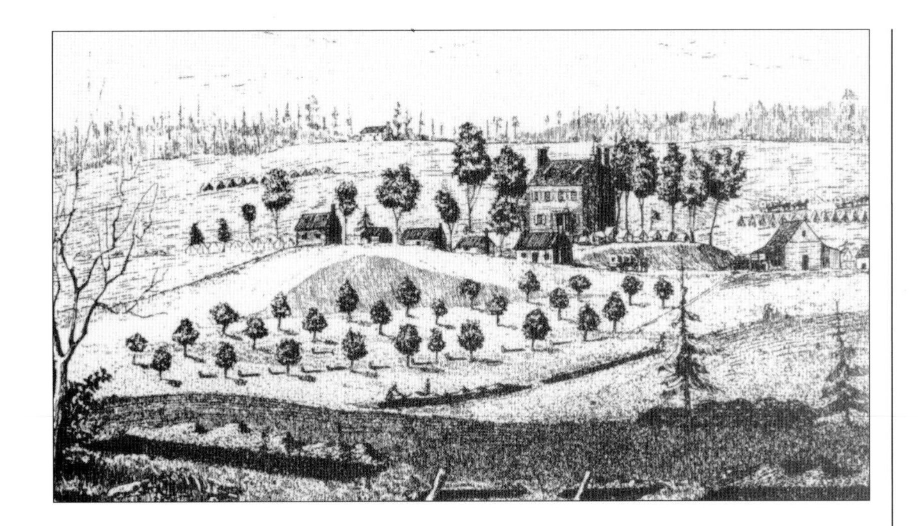

The small railroad halt of Savage's Station on the Richmond & York River Railroad was turned into McClellan's forward supply base south of the Chickahominy River. It also housed the Army of the Potomac's forward field hospital. (Stratford Archive)

Watts House and the Adams House. The French observer the Prince de Joinville wrote: "*The battle of Gaine's Mill is lost. The enemy is advancing on the plain still in the same order … and every minute he was closing in on the confused mass of the Federals … Then came the order for cavalry to charge … I saw the troopers draw their swords with the sudden and electrical impulse of determination and devotion … The charge failed against the dense battalions of the enemy, and the broken regiments galloping through the artillery and flying infantry only increased the general disorder.*" The 400 troopers left over a quarter of their companions behind. Only the arrival of Richardson's Division helped save the day, as these fresh troops deployed into line about 900 yards from the crest, covering the withdrawal of Porter's remaining guns and providing a bastion for his infantry to rally behind.

The battle of Savage's Station, fought on 29 June, was a rearguard action where Sumner's II Corps kept Magruder's Confederates at bay while the rest of the army escaped across the White Oak Swamp. (Stratford Archive)

US

THE CHARGE OF THE 4TH TEXAS AT GAINE'S MILL, 27 JUNE 1862 (pages 50-51)

For much of the day on 27 June, the Union defenders on Turkey Hill had things their own way. However, the arrival of Jackson and Whiting gave Lee the chance to launch a final attack all along the Union line. Just before he launched the attack, Lee rode up to John Hood, with whom he had served on the Texas frontier. The commander asked Hood; "Can you break this line?" Hood replied that he would try. Then, Hood's divisional commander pointed to the Rhode Island battery on Turkey hill (1)**, and ordered that it must be captured. Hood retorted: "I have a regiment that can take it". He meant his old formation, the 4th Texas. When the charge went in, Colonel Marshall led the regiment forward, the men with strict instructions not to fire until ordered. The Union line would be broken by shock, not firepower. Marshall was shot early in the assault, and Lieutenant Colonel Warwick assumed command, carrying the regimental flag himself until he was struck down. The gunners fired into the oncoming wave, but they were unable to halt the attack, the Confederates scrambling down into the defile of Boatswain's Creek** (2)**. This time the defenders broke and scrambled up the hill "like rats from a burning ship" with the Confederates on their heels. Hood led from the front. Over on the Union right flank Jackson's men also surged forward, and drove back the Union line that secured Porter's right flank** (3)**. This meant that the Union batteries and regiments lining the crest of the bluff on Turkey Hill were unsupported, and although the troops had successfully held their ground all day, this had an unsteadying effect. Worse, a wave of Confederate infantry were scrambling up the slope towards with their Rebel Yells rolling in front of them. The Confederates crested the hill, where they were met by the point-blank fire of Lieutenant Buckley's guns** (4)**, which were now stripped of any effective infantry support. Two guns kept firing with three men to each gun as the Union infantry streamed past, by which time Buckley realized his limber horses had been killed, and he was unable to save his guns. The Confederates were almost upon him** (5)**, so he gave his remaining gunners the order to abandon their guns. The Confederates planted their flag** (6) **on one of the guns, an action which electrified the Texans who saw it. The regiment rallied, then launched a second charge that afternoon, against the Union reserve gun line, which was covering Porter's retreat. The 4th Texas had covered itself with glory, but the cost was high. Of the men who began the charge 253 had become casualties, including their Colonel, Lieutenant Colonel, three captains and seven lieutenants. Amazingly the standard bearer emerged unscathed. (Stephen Walsh)**

Many of the Union sick and wounded at Savage's Station field hospital were abandoned during the evening of 29 June when McClellan ordered Sumner's II Corps to join the retreat. This photograph by James Gibson was taken on 28 June. (Library of Congress)

As twilight came the firing dwindled away, and Porter's men were able to withdraw to the safety of the river crossings. It had been a long day, and a costly one. Porter lost 894 men killed, 3,114 wounded, and 2,829 more were captured; a total of 6,837 men or a third of his entire Corps, the largest in the army. Lee's losses were even worse; 1,483 killed, 6,402 wounded and 108 missing: a total of 7,993 men, 1,000 of them lost during the final assault. However, the Confederates now held the north side of the Chickahominy River, McClellan was all but cut off from his supply base, and his Union army was in retreat. It was the bloodiest day of the war so far in the east, but it was the pivotal point of the campaign.

The Union supply depot at Savage's Station, sketched during the afternoon of 27 June. Two days later the base was set alight and abandoned. Watercolor by William McIlvaine Jr. (Military Order of the Loyal Legion of the United States)

RETREAT TO THE JAMES, 28–30 JUNE 1862

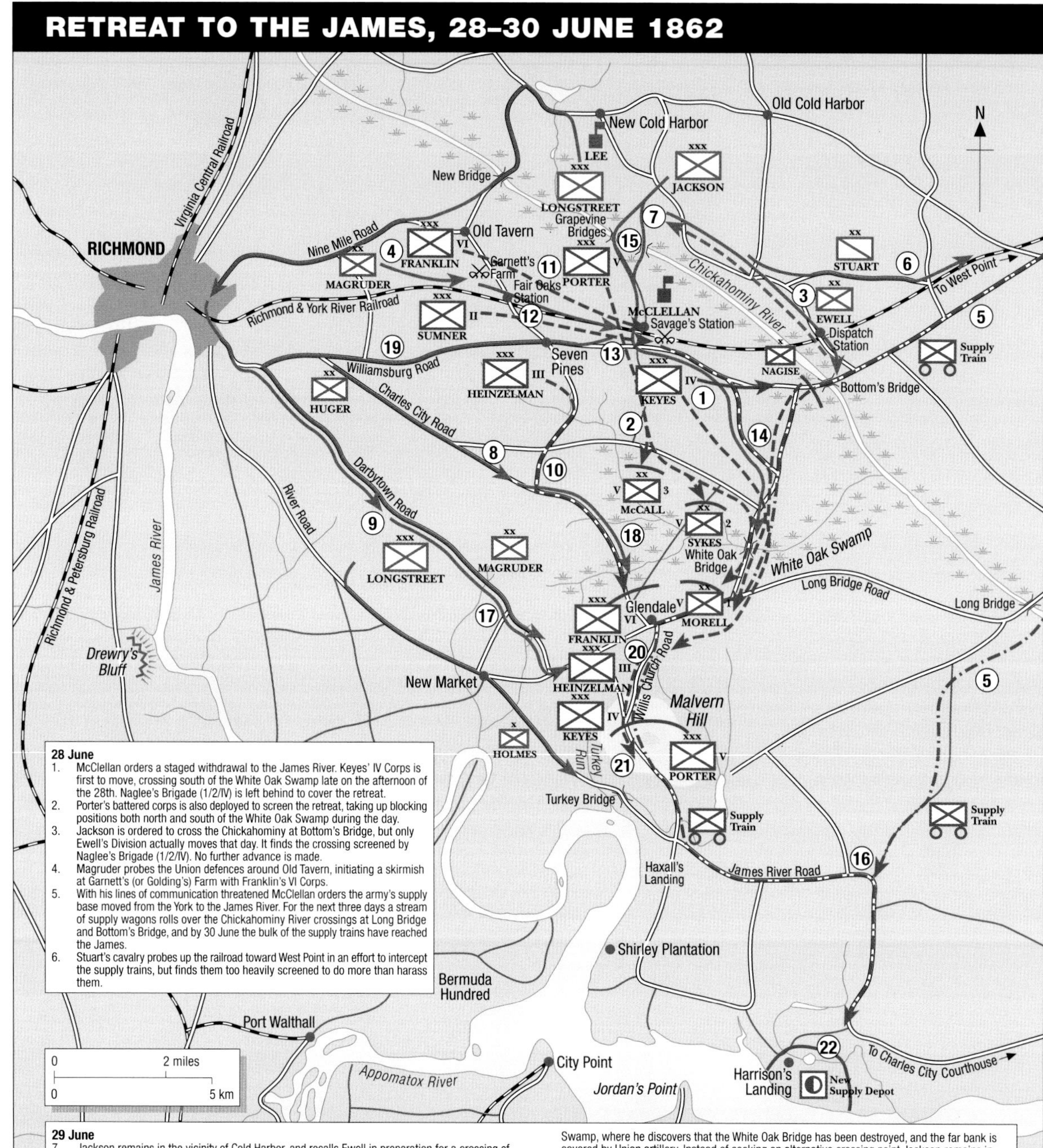

28 June

1. McClellan orders a staged withdrawal to the James River. Keyes' IV Corps is first to move, crossing south of the White Oak Swamp late on the afternoon of the 28th. Naglee's Brigade (1/2/IV) is left behind to cover the retreat.
2. Porter's battered corps is also deployed to screen the retreat, taking up blocking positions both north and south of the White Oak Swamp during the day.
3. Jackson is ordered to cross the Chickahominy at Bottom's Bridge, but only Ewell's Division actually moves that day. It finds the crossing screened by Naglee's Brigade (1/2/IV). No further advance is made.
4. Magruder probes the Union defences around Old Tavern, initiating a skirmish at Garnett's (or Golding's) Farm with Franklin's VI Corps.
5. With his lines of communication threatened McClellan orders the army's supply base moved from the York to the James River. For the next three days a stream of supply wagons rolls over the Chickahominy River crossings at Long Bridge and Bottom's Bridge, and by 30 June the bulk of the supply trains have reached the James.
6. Stuart's cavalry probes up the railroad toward West Point in an effort to intercept the supply trains, but finds them too heavily screened to do more than harass them.

29 June

7. Jackson remains in the vicinity of Cold Harbor, and recalls Ewell in preparation for a crossing of the Grapevine Bridges the following day.
8. Huger slips south down the Charles City Road in an attempt to cut the Union line of retreat off south of White Oak Swamp. He halts when his scouts encounter Union troops deployed northwest of the Glendale crossroads.
9. Lee orders Longstreet to make an even more dramatic outflanking move, and his troops cross the Chickahominy, then skirt Richmond to advance down the Darbytown Road towards Glendale.
10. Heinzelman's III Corps is ordered to move south of the White Oak Swamp, and reaches its new defensive positions in time to prevent Huger's advance down the Charles City Road.
11. Franklin's VI Corps and Sumner's II Corps retire from their defensive positions around Fair Oaks Station and withdraw east toward Savage's Station, where they are expected to hold and screen the rest of the army and its supply trains.
12. Magruder advances to occupy the abandoned fortifications, then pursues the enemy to Savage's Station.
13. Magruder fights a brief but bloody engagement. Sumner manages to halt any further Confederate advance, and Magruder withdraws a little to regroup, easing the pressure on the Union rearguard.
14. McClellan then orders Franklin and Heinzelman to retire in good order across the White Oak Bridge as the last of the wagon trains reach the relative safety of the southern side of White Oak Swamp. Naglee's Brigade is also withdrawn south of the swamp at the same time.

30 June

15. Jackson finally begins his advance, crossing the Chickahominy and advancing as far as White Oak Swamp, where he discovers that the White Oak Bridge has been destroyed, and the far bank is covered by Union artillery. Instead of seeking an alternative crossing point Jackson remains in position, and an artillery duel begins that lasts throughout the day.
16. The last of the Union supply trains cross Bottom's Bridge on the night of 29/30 June, and the final wagons cross over the Long Bridge early the following morning. Throughout the day the last of the Union supply wagons pass through the Glendale crossroads, then down the Willis Church Road to Malvern Hill and the James River Road beyond.
17. Longstreet resumes his advance down the Darbytown road, and when he encounters Union troops around Frayser's Farm he attacks, initiating the battle of Frayser's Farm (or Glendale). He is reinforced by Holmes' Brigade, which he sends down the River Road to probe the area south of Malvern Hill.
18. Huger also joins the attack, using the axis of the Charles City Road to strike the Union lines northwest of the Glendale crossroads
19. Lee orders Magruder to move round to reinforce Longstreet, and his troops spend the day on the march, only reaching the Frayser's Farm battlefield after the fighting has come to an end.
20. McClellan has almost more troops than he has space to deploy them around Frayser's Farm and Glendale, so he orders Porter to take up new defensive positions to the south on Malvern Hill, while Keyes' IV Corps covers the Willis Church Road.
21. Porter reaches Malvern Hill before Holmes, and his position becomes the new rallying point for the army when it resumes its retreat after nightfall.
22. By the evening of 30 June the relocation of the Union supply base from West Point to Harrison's Landing on the James River is complete. With the supply trains safe, McClellan is free to order the withdrawal of his army from its positions along the White Oak Swamp and Frayser's Farm to Malvern Hill and Harrison's Landing, led by Keyes' IV Corps.

After this it would be a tale of Union retreat and Confederate pursuit, all the way to the James.

THE RETREAT

On the evening of 27 June McClellan sent a telegram to Secretary of War Stanton. It reported: "*Attacked by greatly superior numbers in all directions on this side. We still hold our own, though a heavy fire is still kept up on the bank of the Chickahominy. The odds have been immense. We hold our own very nearly. I may be forced to give up my position during the night ... Had I 20,000 fresh and good troops we would be sure of a splendid victory tomorrow.*" Amazingly this hinted that Magruder had attacked south of the Chickahominy, but apart from a heavy skirmish between Franklin's VII Corps and Magruder's men at Garnett's Farm near Old Tavern, no such engagement had taken place. McClellan called a meeting that evening at the Trent House, attended by Keyes, Franklin, Sumner, the Prince de Joinville, and even the weary Porter. It was decided that the army should retreat, and McClellan immediately ordered his headquarters staff to move south to Savage's Station. The retreat had begun. Shortly after midnight McClellan sent another telegram to Stanton: "*I know now the full history of the day. On this side of the river we repulsed several strong attacks. On the left bank our men ... were overwhelmed by vastly superior numbers ... I have not a man in reserve, and shall be glad to cover my retreat and save the material and personnel of the army ... I have lost this battle because my force was too small. I again repeat that I am not responsible for this.*" Even more amazingly, he finished this

When the order came to retreat south of the Chickahominy River, Union troops at Savage's Station set about destroying all the rolling stock they could. The railroad bridge of the Chickahominy River had already been destroyed, so this burning ammunition train was allowed to freewheel down the line and crash into the river. Sketch by Alfred Waud. (Library of Congress)

Once all Union troops had crossed White Oak Swamp Bridge to safety, Brigadier General Smith, commanding the Union division at White Oak Swamp, ordered the bridge to be destroyed, in an effort to impede Jackson's advance. (Stratford Archive)

defeatist message with a direct attack against Stanton and Lincoln: *"If I save this army now, I tell you plainly that I owe no thanks to you, or any other person in Washington. You have done your best to sacrifice this army."* This ranks as one of the most bizarre communiqués of the war, and betrays the complete collapse of McClellan's confidence. From this point on he would be obsessed with saving his army from Lee's countless hordes.

For his part Lee was perplexed as to the whereabouts of McClellan's army. At dawn on 28 June he sent J.E.B. Stuart's cavalry and Richard Ewell's Division down the Cold Harbor Road towards the Richmond & York River Railroad near Dispatch Station, where he confidently expected to find the bulk of the Army of the Potomac, drawn up to protect their lines of supply. By noon the word came back that the area was clear of enemy troops, and even more surprisingly the railroad bridge over the Chickahominy River had been burned. This meant that McClellan's supply line to White House was severed. Stuart was dispatched eastward up the railroad to find out what was happening, while Lee pondered his next move. Clearly his grand strategy had fallen apart, as McClellan had not behaved as Lee had expected. This meant the entire Army of the Potomac was probably constricted into its lines between the Chickahominy River and the White Oak Swamp. South of this, both sides had thin picket lines stretching to the James River. Lee was unable to comprehend that any commander would simply abandon his supply base so easily, and was wary that McClellan might be planning some kind of trap. He was giving the Union commander more credit than he deserved. It was only the following morning (29 June) when Stuart's men rode into the smoldering remains of the Union supply depot at White House that the full enormity of McClellan's move was brought home to Lee. While riders were sent back to headquarters with the news, the Confederate cavalry explored the burned camp. The Southern troopers were amazed that the invaders brought supplies of tinned fish to stack beside a river that was teeming with fish! Less amusingly, Robert E. Lee's son Colonel Rooney Lee picked over the smoldering remains of his family estate, the historic White House, which had once been the home of George Washington's wife. Colonel Martin

Union artillery from Franklin's VI Corps conduct counter-battery fire against Jackson's guns on the far bank of White Oak Swamp during the afternoon of 30 June. Sketch by Alfred Waud. (Library of Congress)

wrote: *"This once beautiful estate … now utterly despoiled, forcibly reminded us that we were contending against a foe respecting nothing, sparing nothing."*

Away to the west, Rooney's father had devised another plan. This time he was not content with maneuvering the enemy away from Richmond. This time Lee hoped to be able to trap the Army of the Potomac against the James River and destroy it. Had Lee succeeded the war could well have ended that summer. There was little action on the part of the Confederates on 29 June, as Lee busied himself by giving all his scattered divisions new orders. His plan called for Jackson to cross the Chicka-hominy River at Grapevine Bridge, then to advance on Savage's Station. If the enemy was still in retreat, he would move southeast toward the bridge crossing the White Oak Swamp. Longstreet would cross over the river at either New Bridge or Mechanicsville, then advance down the Darbytown Road to reach a position south of the White Oak Swamp. Similarly Magruder, after pressing the enemy to his front, would disengage and join Longstreet in the area between the White Oak Swamp and the James River Road. Huger would advance almost due east along the Charles City Road, driving the enemy before him. The aim was to pin the Union army in their area around Glendale, south of the White Oak Swamp, but far enough from the James River that the union gunboats there would be unable to support McClellan's army. Finally, General Holmes with his North Carolinians would move through Richmond, then down the New Market Road and River Road to cut McClellan off from the James River. It was an ambitious plan, and relied on a level of staff work that, at that stage of the war, simply did not exist in the Army of Northern Virginia. Longstreet had already demonstrated his ability to get lost in the same area during the battle of Fair Oaks the previous month, while Jackson had already placed Lee's campaign in jeopardy with his tardiness. The only guarantee in the coming days was that it would be Lee rather than McClellan who would control the pace and flow of the campaign.

On the morning of 28 June, Keyes' IV Corps began its withdrawal over the White Oak Swamp via the White Oak Road, followed at around noon by Porter's battered V Corps. Slocum's Division of Franklin's VI Corps was also ordered to White Oak Swamp to cover the withdrawal of the army's supply wagons. Smith's Division remained behind to guard

McClellan's supply wagons approach White Oak Swamp, 28 June. This detail of a contemporary lithograph captures something of the scale of the logistical operation, which involved over 4,000 supply wagons. (Library of Congress)

against any advance by Magruder, together with Heintzelman's III Corps and Sumner's II Corps. McClellan's plan was for these remaining formations to withdraw during the night of 28/29 June. Meanwhile, over 4,000 wagons would roll south over the Chickahominy by way of several bridges to reach the safety of Harrison's Landing. By late afternoon IV Corps and Morell's Division of Porter's V Corps had managed to cross the White Oak Swamp Bridge, but the remaining two divisions of V Corps were held up by the line of supply wagons making the same crossing, and in late afternoon they made camp north of the Swamp, ready to cross the bridge early the following morning. However, the withdrawal of part of Franklin's VI Corps was delayed when Magruder launched another limited attack in the vicinity of Garnett's Farm during 28 June. He probed Smith's Division deployed around the Golding Farm, covering the road between Grapevine Bridge and Savage's Station that Porter's Corps had marched down. A sharp firefight developed, during which the Georgian brigades of George T. Anderson and Robert Toombs suffered heavy losses, forcing them to withdraw. This was the only threat posed to McClellan's army during the entire day, but it helped reinforce his notion that the Confederates were about to launch a large-scale attack from the west.

Major General Benjamin Huger (1805–77) advanced too slowly to join Longstreet's assault at Frayser's Farm on 30 June, and was therefore responsible for squandering one of the few opportunities for the Confederates to crush the Army of the Potomac. (Library of Congress)

On the morning of Sunday 29 June, Lee ordered Magruder to advance with all three of his divisions, heading east along the Williamsburg Road toward Savage's Station. Scouts reported that the position held by Smith's Division had been abandoned during the night, and within an hour it was discovered that the same was true all along the line of Union earthworks stretching from the Chickahominy River to the White Oak Swamp. The threat to Richmond had been lifted. Magruder began his advance, while Huger marched southeast down the Charles City Road to intercept McClellan's line of retreat around Glendale. Lee was improvising all the time. Ewell and Stuart remained north of the Chickahominy River in case McClellan's tried to head east down the Peninsula. The three Richmond divisions of Longstreet and the two Hills were still encamped beside the Gaine's Mill battlefield, and that morning set off on their long, circular route to intercept the Army of the Potomac between the White Oak Swamp and the James River. This meant that the only portion of the Confederate army that had a chance of catching McClellan that day was Magruder's force of three small divisions.

THE BATTLE OF SAVAGE'S STATION

Lee accompanied Magruder as far as Fair Oaks Station, then rode off to find Huger. That morning Magruder was in poor health, and had taken morphine to combat his chronic indigestion. He was in no condition to fight a battle, but at least the morale of his troops was high, while Union morale continued to plummet as the army abandoned its stores and even its wounded. Smoke from burning stores marked the line of retreat to the White Oak Swamp Bridge. That morning McClellan's rearguard consisted of Sumner's II Corps and Heintzelman's III Corps, supported by Smith's Division of Franklin's VI Corps. No single corps commander was in overall charge. Shortly after 9.00am, G.T. Anderson's brigade encountered part of the Union rearguard near the Allen Farm on the Williamsburg Road, part of Israel Richardson's Division of II Corps. The fighting lasted for two hours, giving the Union rearguard time to prepare a line of defense around Savage's Station, where according to Surgeon Stevens, *"trains and troops were crowded together in wonderful confusion."* For his part Magruder was convinced he was about to be attacked, and begged for assistance from Huger. Lee had hoped that Jackson would be able to cross the Grapevine Bridge to increase the pressure on McClellan's rearguard, but due to confusion over orders and the need to rebuild the river crossing, Jackson's men remained north of the Chickahominy River throughout the day. Around noon, III Corps pulled out of the Union line and began its march to the White Oak Swamp Bridge. Heintzelman never bothered to tell Sumner of his withdrawal. It was 5.00pm before Magruder resumed his advance, sending almost three brigades down the Williamsburg Road, then deploying them into line: Joseph Kershaw on the left, Paul Semmes in the centre and Richard Griffith on the right. In support Magruder employed the first ever railway-gun, an improvised affair that followed the troops down the railroad and then lobbed shells at Savage's Station. The Confederates advanced, encountering William Burns' Brigade, supported on its left flank by William Brooks' Brigade. The Confederate

Major General Theophilus H. Holmes (1804-80) was ordered to lead his North Carolinian Division along the River Road to cut McClellan's retreat to the James River. Union gunboats delayed his advance, and he arrived too late to intervene at Malvern Hill or to prevent the Union retreat to Harrison's Landing. (Stratford Archive)

Confederates from Charles Field's Brigade of A.P. Hill's Division charge McCall's Division at the battle of Frayser's Farm, 30 June. Two Union batteries were captured in the action; the same guns that had fired on Field's troops just four days before at Mechanicsville. (Stratford Archive)

attack faltered, although Kershaw's Brigade continued to press forward south of the Williamsburg Road. Rather than passively hold his ground Sumner launched a series of counterattacks against the Confederate center, which had driven Burns back beyond the edge of the woods overlooking the Savage's Station clearing. Although fresh Union regiments were fed into the fight, no real headway was made until nightfall, when Kershaw's South Carolinians were forced to withdraw. Meanwhile behind the Union line, fires raged around the Station as stores and rolling stock were destroyed. During the day, Sumner lost some 1,038 men and Magruder 473, although when the Union army eventually withdrew that night, a further 2,500 wounded were abandoned at the Savage's Station Field Hospital by order of McClellan. After dark, Sumner received orders *"to follow the retreat of the main body of the army."* Sumner and his men were disgusted; having held the enemy all day, they were now expected to abandon the wounded and retreat. Lee was disappointed with Magruder's performance, writing a note to him that read: *"I regret much that you have made so little progress in the pursuit of the enemy. I must urge you then to press on his rear rapidly and vigorously."* However, the reasons for the failure to catch McClellan's army as it retreated lay more in the inadequacies of Confederate staff work than in the limitations of any individual commander. By the following morning Sumner's men were safely across the White Oak Swamp, and as the last Union troops crossed, the bridge was destroyed to hinder any pursuit.

Union artillery in action during the battle of Malvern Hill. Porter's guns were able to silence any Confederate guns ranged against them during 1 July. The piece shown in this engraving is a 12-pdr "Napoleon" smoothbore. (Stratford Archive)

The battle of Malvern Hill, 30 June 1862. The Union guns were able to blow huge gaps in the ranks of the advancing Confederates, and halt their charge before the attackers reached the artillery. Painting by Alfred Ward. (Private Collection)

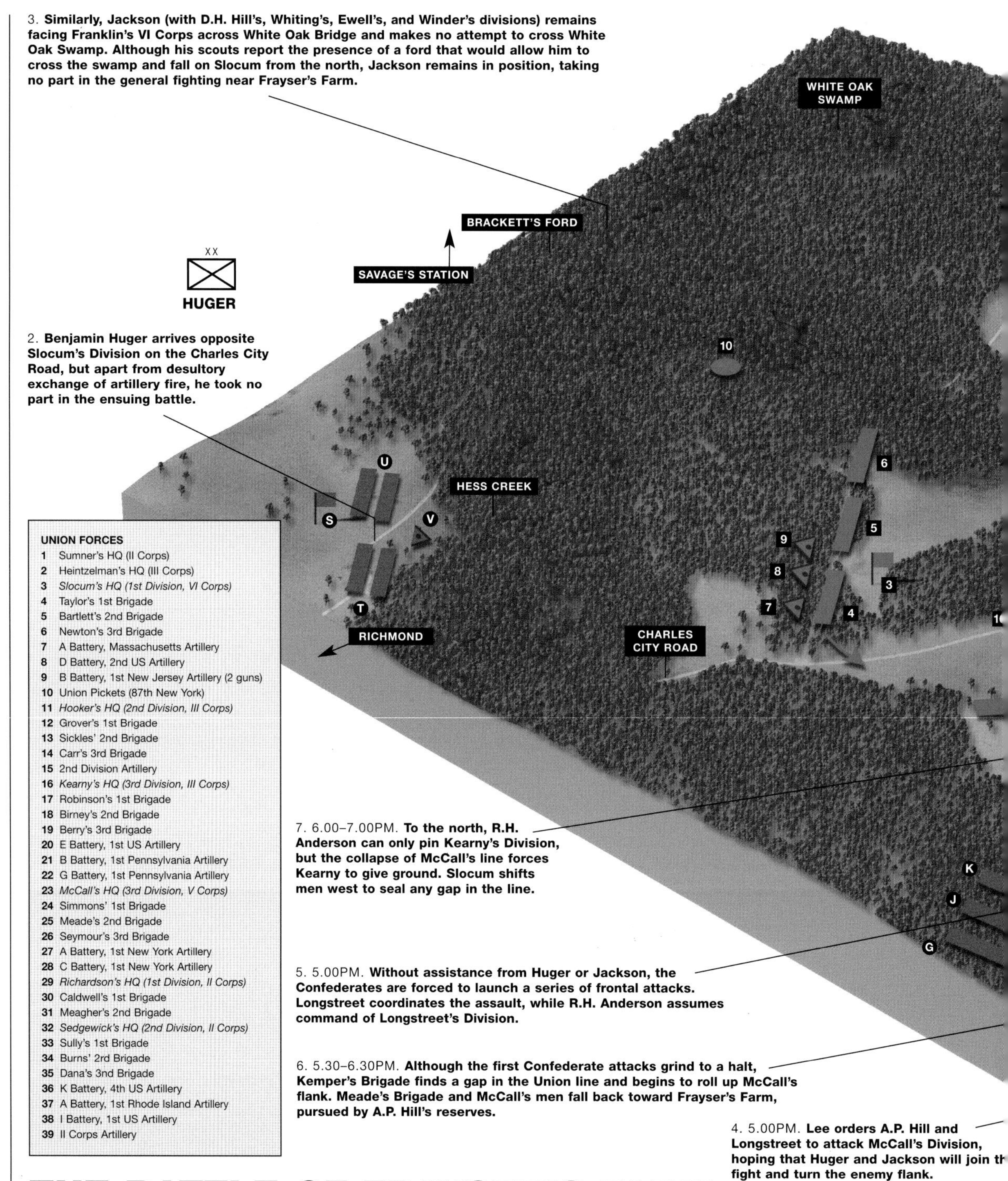

THE BATTLE OF FRAYSER'S FARM

30 June 1862, viewed from the southwest. As McClellan withdraws his army southward toward the James River, he is able to protect his rear by defending the line of the White Oak Swamp. With the rest of Lee's army approaching from the west, he is forced to make a stand near Frayser's Farm, buying time for his supply wagons to roll through Glendale toward his new supply base at Harrison's Landing. Lee is presented with an opportunity to cut the Army of the Potomac off from the safety of the James in the battle of Frayser's Farm (also known as Glendale).

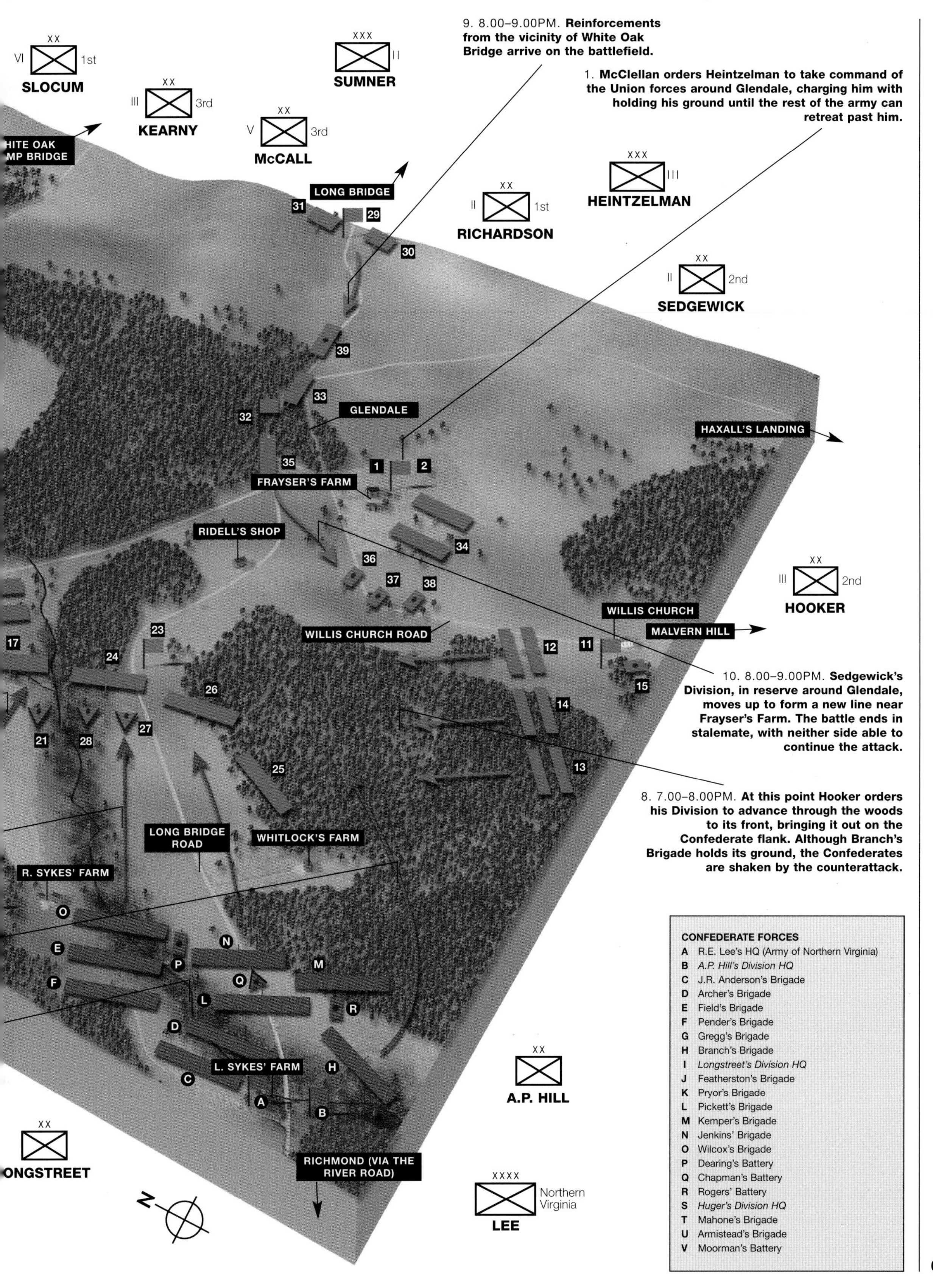
XX
VI 1st
SLOCUM
XX
III 3rd
KEARNY
XX
V 3rd
McCALL
XXX
II
SUMNER
9. 8.00–9.00PM. **Reinforcements from the vicinity of White Oak Bridge arrive on the battlefield.**
1. **McClellan orders Heintzelman to take command of the Union forces around Glendale, charging him with holding his ground until the rest of the army can retreat past him.**
XXX
III
HEINTZELMAN
XX
II 1st
RICHARDSON
XX
II 2nd
SEDGEWICK
HITE OAK
MP BRIDGE
LONG BRIDGE
GLENDALE
FRAYSER'S FARM
RIDELL'S SHOP
HAXALL'S LANDING
XX
III 2nd
HOOKER
WILLIS CHURCH
MALVERN HILL
WILLIS CHURCH ROAD
10. 8.00–9.00PM. **Sedgewick's Division, in reserve around Glendale, moves up to form a new line near Frayser's Farm. The battle ends in stalemate, with neither side able to continue the attack.**
8. 7.00–8.00PM. **At this point Hooker orders his Division to advance through the woods to its front, bringing it out on the Confederate flank. Although Branch's Brigade holds its ground, the Confederates are shaken by the counterattack.**
LONG BRIDGE ROAD
WHITLOCK'S FARM
R. SYKES' FARM
L. SYKES' FARM
RICHMOND (VIA THE RIVER ROAD)
XX
A.P. HILL
XX
ONGSTREET
XXXX
Northern Virginia
LEE
CONFEDERATE FORCES
A R.E. Lee's HQ (Army of Northern Virginia)
B *A.P. Hill's Division HQ*
C J.R. Anderson's Brigade
D Archer's Brigade
E Field's Brigade
F Pender's Brigade
G Gregg's Brigade
H Branch's Brigade
I *Longstreet's Division HQ*
J Featherston's Brigade
K Pryor's Brigade
L Pickett's Brigade
M Kemper's Brigade
N Jenkins' Brigade
O Wilcox's Brigade
P Dearing's Battery
Q Chapman's Battery
R Rogers' Battery
S *Huger's Division HQ*
T Mahone's Brigade
U Armistead's Brigade
V Moorman's Battery

The battlefield from Malvern Hill, viewed from the area where Magruder's advance was halted, some 300 yards short of the Union lines. The Union guns were sited a little behind the two slave cabins on the left of the picture. (Stratford Archive)

FRAYSER'S FARM/GLENDALE

By the morning of 30 June, the Army of the Potomac occupied a curving line stretching roughly southwest to northeast. It ran from Malvern Hill in the south, through the crossroads at Glendale then up to the White Oak Swamp, where it curved along its southern bank to the remains of the bridge. All of the supply wagons were now south of the White Oak Swamp, and the rear of this column had spent the night around Glendale, and would spend the day rolling south to Harrison's Landing. Franklin's VI Corps held the northern portion of the line, supported at White Oak Swamp Bridge by Richardson's Division from II Corps. To the west of Glendale, Heintzelman's III Corps, supported by McCall's and Sedgwick's divisions (from V and II Corps respectively), covered two converging roads; the Long Bridge Road (an extension of the Darbytown Road) to the southwest, and the Charles City Road to the northwest. Unfortunately, Glendale had become a bottleneck, and it would take time to extricate the mass of wagons, guns and troops that clogged the roads. This meant that McClellan's troops would have to make a stand against Lee's Divisions, which were converging on the Glendale crossroads. Longstreet was moving down the Darbytown Road while Huger approached the Union position along the Charles City Road. Holmes, having moved up from south of the James River, was advancing down the New Market Road toward Malvern Hill, in an attempt to cut off the Army of the Potomac from the James River. Lee expected to deal a decisive blow against the enemy around Glendale, but Huger's timidity, Jackson's tardy advance and, again, poor staff work all conspired to deprive him of his victory. Huger would play little part in the coming battle, as he made slow progress down the Charles City Road, and only reached the battlefield in the late afternoon. He then spent the remaining hours before nightfall engaged in an artillery duel with the guns of Slocum's Division. Jackson had eventually crossed the Chickahominy River and by noon his leading units approached the White Oak Swamp Bridge. Rather than forcing a crossing, which could have resulted in heavy casualties, Jackson deployed his artillery and at 2.00pm he began to bombard the southern bank. After leading a reconnaissance of the river crossing Jackson ordered the bombardment to continue then, exhausted, he retired to his headquarters and fell asleep under a tree. In fact, Jackson could well have forced a crossing of the swamp further to the west and, with the aid of Huger, he could have

The advance of Brigadier General Lewis A. Armistead (1817–63) and his Virginian brigade was the signal to launch the first full-scale infantry assault against the Union defenses at Malvern Hill. He survived the battle, but was killed at the head of his men at the climax of Pickett's charge on the final day of the battle of Gettysburg almost exactly a year later. (Stratford Archive)

Malvern Hill dominated the River Road (seen in the middle distance in this view south from Malvern House). The hill was just over a mile from the banks of the James River, where Union gunboats were able to provide gunfire support for McClellan's troops. This watercolor by William McIlvaine Jr. was painted on 30 June. (Military Order of the Loyal Legion of the United States)

put intense pressure on Franklin's overstretched line. Instead, the opportunity was wasted and Jackson only crossed the White Oak Swamp the following day. D.H. Hill's Division was still on the Darbytown Road, and would not reach Glendale before nightfall. On the River Road Holmes came under fire from a flotilla of Union gunboats: *"throwing those awe-inspiring shells familiarly called by our men lampposts."* Holmes, who was deaf, did not hear anything from his command post, but when summoned had to concede his route was effectively blocked. His troops would spend the rest of the day finding a safer route to the east. This left the task of crushing McClellan to Longstreet and A.P. Hill.

The Union base at Harrison's Landing. The army reached the safety of this well-defended riverside base on 2 July, and the troops remained there for a month before the Army of the Potomac was transported away from the Virginia Peninsula. (Stratford Archive)

Porter's V Corps was the last portion of the Army of the Potomac to reach the safety of Harrison's Landing on the evening of 2 July. This sketch shows the massed campfires of the troops already encamped by the James River. (Library of Congress)

Six Union Divisions were deployed in the vicinity of Glendale and Frayser's Farm (also known as the Nelson Farm), a dwelling on the Willis Church Road that McClellan used as a headquarters. Blocking the Confederate advance up the Long Bridge Road was McCall's 3rd Division of V Corps, supported on the right by Kearny' 3rd Division and the left by Hooker's 2nd Division, both part of Heintzelman's III Corps. Further to the north, Slocum's 1st Division of VI Corps covered the Charles City Road in case Huger made an appearance. Two divisions of Sumner's

To cover his nocturnal withdrawal during the early hours of 2 July, Porter left behind a line of dummy "quaker guns" and scarecrow sentries on top of Malvern Hill – part of a ruse to delay any Confederate pursuit. In fact the Confederates were too badly battered the previous day to chase Porter, and the Southern troops spent the day burying the dead. (Stratford Archive)

In this contemporary cartoon McClellan is shown relaxing on board the USS *Galena* off Harrison's Landing during the afternoon of 1 July while his army was fighting at Malvern Hill. (Stratford Archive)

II Corps (Richardson's 1st and Sedgwick's 2nd) were held in reserve in the fields immediately west of the Willis Church Road.

Longstreet and A.P. Hill were in position by 11.00am, but Lee held them back until he heard firing from Huger, or Jackson's columns. The firing never came. At one stage President Jefferson Davis appeared, and together with Lee he rode forward to inspect the Union lines. They were fired on, and in Longstreet's words; *"Our little party speedily retired to safer quarters. The Federals doubtless had no idea that the Confederate President, commanding general and divisional commanders were receiving point-blank shot from their batteries."* At 5.00pm, Lee had given up any hope of his other two columns on the Charles City Road and White Oak Swamp Road, so he ordered Longstreet to begin his attack, advancing northeast along the line of the Long Bridge Road toward the Glendale crossroads. The experienced brigades of Wilcox, Jenkins, and Kemper led the assault on McCall's line. These were the Union troops who had defended their positions at Mechanicsville and Gaine's Mill, but the sudden assault of Longstreet's men proved too much. Seymour's Brigade on the left of McCall's line was broken, and two artillery batteries were overrun. Private Urban of the 1st Pennsylvania remembered that: *"We were compelled to fall back in confusion to the edge of the wood in the rear of Cooper's Battery"*. On the Federal right, Wilcox managed to push back Meade's Brigade. McCall's reserve brigade under Simmons (formerly Reynold's Brigade) counterattacked, but ultimately failed to prevent the Division being driven back almost to the Glendale Junction. R.H. Anderson led forward the second wave of Confederates; the brigades of Featherstone, Pryor, and Hunton (formerly Pickett's Brigade), together with Field's Brigade from A.P. Hill's Division. Anderson swung his men to the left, slamming into the left flank of Kearny's Division, deployed in the woods to the north of McCall. Sumner fed reinforcements into the battle along the Charles City Road, and eventually Anderson was halted. The inactivity of Huger also meant that part of Slocum's Division could be redeployed to face the Confederate assault. On the southern edge of the battlefield, a small creek marked the boundary of McCall's position, and Branch's Brigade of A.P. Hill's Division advanced into the woods lining

Union gunboats on the James River fire in support of the army during the battle of Malvern Hill, 1 July. The two vessels shown are the ironclad screw gunboat USS *Galena* (left) and the wooden sidewheel gunboat USS *Mahaska* (right). (Museum of Fine Arts, Boston, MA)

the stream, encountering no resistance as it advanced. However, as Branch's North Carolinians emerged from the woods they ran into the brigades of Cuvier Grover of Hooker's Division and the men of William Burns' Brigade, part of Sedgwick's Division, in front of the Willis Church. Branch pulled back into the safety of the woods. In the center the collapse of McCall's Division created a temporary crisis, but Sedgwick held his ground, then launched a limited series of counter-attacks around Ridell's Shop, a shack on the Charles City Road that found itself in the midst of the fighting. Longstreet later wrote: *"Ten thousand of A.P. Hill's Division had been held in reserve in the hope that Jackson and Huger would come up on our left, enabling us to dislodge the Federals, after which Hill's troops could be put in fresh to give pursuit and follow them down to Harrison's Landing ... As neither Jackson nor Huger came up, and as night drew on, I put Hill in to relieve my troops."* A.P. Hill led the remaining Confederate brigades into the fighting, but he was unable to break through, despite witnessing the rout of the Union division that had humiliated him at Mechanicsville just four days before, and the capture of its commander. As dusk fell the Union defenders fell back slightly, but as Longstreet put it: "*As the enemy moved off they continued the fire of their artillery upon us from various points, and it was after 9 'o'clock when the shells ceased to fall.*" Darkness brought an end to the fighting.

At Frayser's Farm Lee lost some 638 men killed, 2,814 wounded and another 221 missing. McClellan lost 297 men killed, 1,696 men wounded and 1,804 missing. Each side lost just over 3,500 men. It was a costly battle, but for once luck had been on the side of McClellan. Lee had failed to crush the Union army, and McClellan was able to continue his retreat. It had been Lee's one big chance for a decisive victory, and the opportunity was wasted. Although the two sides would meet again the following day, the critical moment had passed.

The Berkley Plantation served as McClellan's headquarters during his army's sojourn at Harrison's Landing. (Author's photograph)

Boatswain's Creek lay at the bottom of a flat-bottomed defile that was not marked on Confederate maps. The creek therefore served as an unexpected obstacle to the attackers during the battle of Gaine's Mill, and by the end of 27 June it was clogged with bodies. (Author's photograph)

MALVERN HILL

Although the Union army made good use of terrain during the Seven Days – the defensive positions behind Beaver Dam Creek and Boatswain's Creek were both formidable – the Army of the Potomac never occupied a better defensive position than Malvern Hill. The hill was actually a broad plateau, a mile north of the James River with its base on the River Road (New Market Road). A steep bluff known as the Malvern Hill Cliffs protected the western side of the plateau, while to the right the swampy ground of Turkey Island Creek also favored the defender. The Carter's Mill Road bisected the plateau and the Willis Church Road, running in southwest from Glendale crossroads, intersected the Carter's Mill Road on the northern edge of the plateau. The latter continued on to join the River Road by the James River, where union gunboats were providing covering fire. Any attacker would have to cross the open space of the plateau, and advance into the teeth of McClellan's guns. It was an ideal position from which to cover the army's retreat. McClellan sent Keyes' IV Corps on to Harrison's Landing, and drew the rest of the army up in a defensive position on Malvern Hill. Once again, Porter was given the task of holding the front line, largely because he was the first Union Corps commander to reach the hill early on the morning of 30 June. Porter deployed the army's artillery reserve where it could cover the western approaches to the hill along the River Road. These batteries and the Union gunboats on the river would be sufficient to deter Holmes from advancing to threaten the army's rear. Porter's own V Corps was drawn up to the left of the Carter's Mill Road, facing north, while Heintzelman's III Corps deployed on his right, on

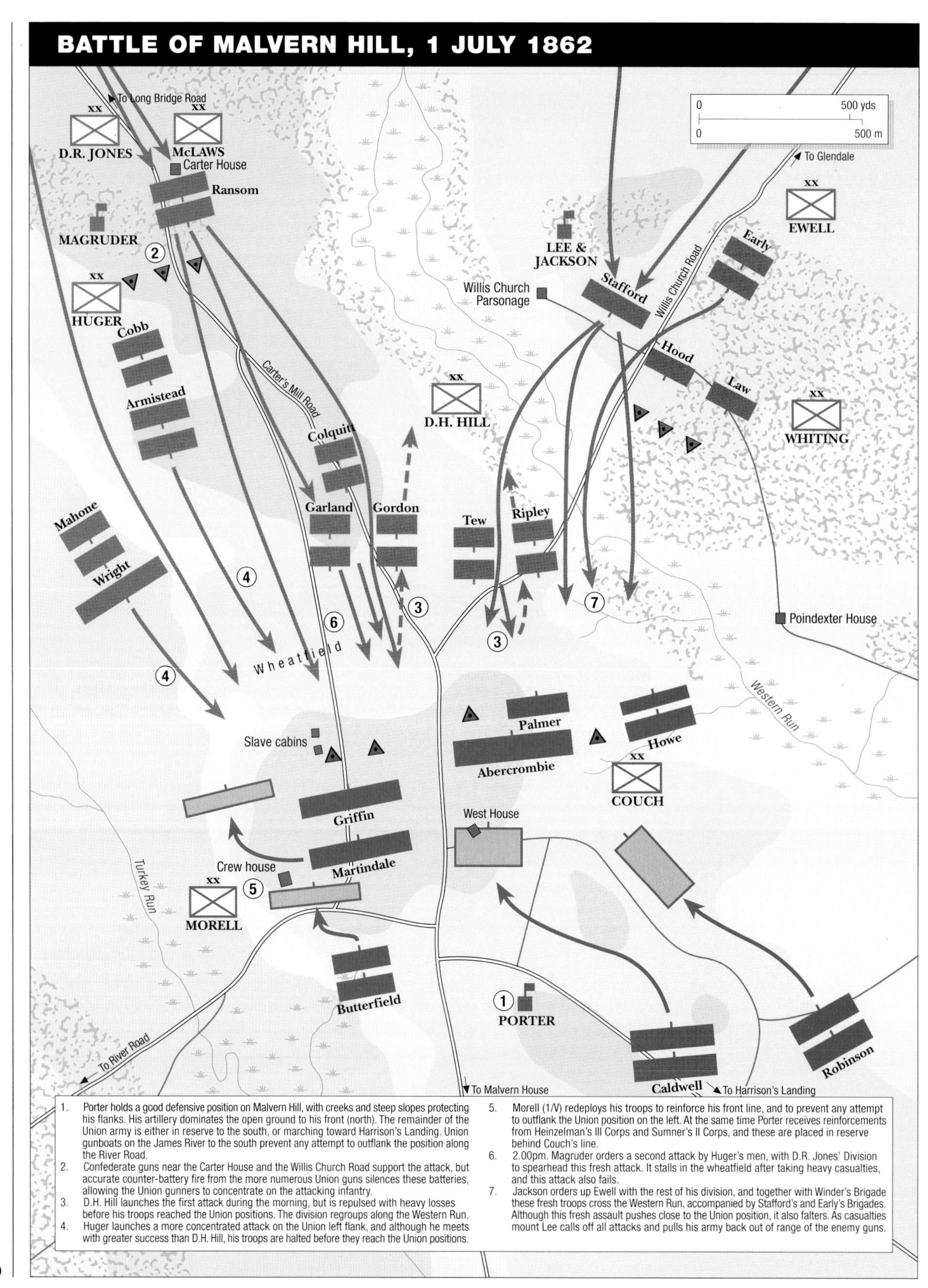

1. Porter holds a good defensive position on Malvern Hill, with creeks and steep slopes protecting his flanks. His artillery dominates the open ground to his front (north). The remainder of the Union army is either in reserve to the south, or marching toward Harrison's Landing. Union gunboats on the James River to the south prevent any attempt to outflank the position along the River Road.
2. Confederate guns near the Carter House and the Willis Church Road support the attack, but accurate counter-battery fire from the more numerous Union guns silences these batteries, allowing the Union gunners to concentrate on the attacking infantry.
3. D.H. Hill launches the first attack during the morning, but is repulsed with heavy losses before his troops reached the Union positions. The division regroups along the Western Run.
4. Huger launches a more concentrated attack on the Union left flank, and although he meets with greater success than D.H. Hill, his troops are halted before they reach the Union positions.
5. Morell (1/V) redeploys his troops to reinforce his front line, and to prevent any attempt to outflank the Union position on the left. At the same time Porter receives reinforcements from Heinzelman's III Corps and Sumner's II Corps, and these are placed in reserve behind Couch's line.
6. 2.00pm. Magruder orders a second attack by Huger's men, with D.R. Jones' Division to spearhead this fresh attack. It stalls in the wheatfield after taking heavy casualties, and this attack also fails.
7. Jackson orders up Ewell with the rest of his division, and together with Winder's Brigade these fresh troops cross the Western Run, accompanied by Stafford's and Early's Brigades. Although this fresh assault pushes close to the Union position, it also falters. As casualties mount Lee calls off all attacks and pulls his army back out of range of the enemy guns.

The Watts House at Gaine's Mill lay immediately behind Morell's divisional line running along the top of the southern crest of the Boatswain's Creek defile. Porter established his headquarters beside the dwelling. (Author's photograph)

the eastern side of the plateau. Sumner's II Corps lay in reserve behind the front line, while Franklin's VI Corps deployed further east, protecting the army's flank and its line of retreat. The entire front was covered with artillery and skirmishers, while the infantry took up their positions behind the guns. This was a killing ground, and Porter was determined to use his guns to best advantage. A half mile to the rear, the siege guns that had made the journey from the White House deployed around the Malvern Hill House, which was used as a hospital. As the army commander, McClellan should have controlled the battle, but after supervising the deployment of his army the general had embarked on the ironclad USS *Galena* early that morning, and was anchored off Harrison's Landing when the battle took place.

Shortly after dawn, Robert E. Lee met Magruder, Longstreet, A.P. Hill, D.H. Hill, and Jackson. At last he had all his commanders in one

This line of guns marks the location where Porter deployed the bulk of his artillery west of Carter's Mill Road on Malvern Hill. The two slave cabins were located immediately forward of the left-hand gun, and the battery points toward the slight elevation where Lee and Longstreet placed their right flank "grand battery". (Author's photograph)

ABOVE **This monument to Cadmus Wilcox marks the spot where he fell leading his Alabama brigade against Porter's left flank, on the southern slopes of the Boatswain's Creek defile. This sector of the Union front was held by Butterfield's Brigade. (Author's photograph)**

ABOVE, LEFT **The remains of Willis Church Parsonage on the Willis Church Road. Lee established his headquarters near the parsonage during the battle of Malvern Hill on 1 July. (Author's photograph)**

place, with the exception of Huger and Holmes. Lee was feeling unwell that morning, so he asked Longstreet to act as his understudy in case he had to retire from the field. Longstreet duly turned his division over to R.H. Anderson and joined Lee's staff. He ordered Jackson to march down by Willis Church Road from Glendale, followed by Magruder. Huger was ordered to work his way south along a lane running from Glendale to the Carter Farm toward Malvern Hill, while A.P. Hill advanced down the Carter's Mill Road, followed by D.H. Hill. Unfortunately Magruder began marching down the wrong road, and it took Longstreet three hours to find his missing three divisions, and guide them back toward the battle. For once it was Jackson who was first to arrive in front of the Union positions. He deployed on the Confederate left flank, to the east of the Willis Church Road, and deployed his guns so they could concentrate their fire on the centre of Porter's line. D.H. Hill deployed on Jackson's right, his left flank anchored on the Willis Church Road. Immediately behind the Confederate front line, Lee established his headquarters close to the Willis Church Parsonage. Lewis Armistead's and Ambrose Wright's brigades from Huger's Division deployed on D.H. Hill's right flank, a position that had been earmarked for the missing Magruder. Lee and Longstreet found a good site for the guns just in front of the Carter Farm, where a slight elevation gave them a clear line of fire across the dip in the plateau toward Porter's left flank to the southeast. He decided to use a "grand battery" to pound the Union guns into submission, and then launch his infantry into an attack all along the front. Unfortunately for him it would be Porter whose artillery had the best of the coming exchange. Lee returned to his headquarters, and Longstreet remained on the high ground to supervise the deployment of troops and the barrage. The first batteries opened fire, and were soon answered by the larger shells of the Union guns, supported by the siege pieces. It was an unequal contest. Only 16 Confederate guns could be brought into action from Jackson's command, and they were soon silenced by the

OPPOSITE **Like the Chickahominy River, the White Oak Swamp was an impenetrable mass of marsh, river, and wetland. This photograph was taken at the location of the White Oak Swamp Bridge where Jackson wasted most of 30 June. Unknown to him a second crossing at Brackett's Ford lay just three miles to the west. (Author's photograph)**

UNION ARTILLERY AT THE BATTLE OF MALVERN HILL, 1 JULY 1862 (pages 74-75)

In order to cover the retreat of the Union army to Harrison's Landing, Porter elected to stand and fight on Malvern Hill, a superb but deceptive defensive position close to the James River. The rear of the hill was covered by the overwhelming firepower of the Union fleet, while Porter's flanks were protected by a cliff on one side and a marshy swamp on the other. If Lee was going to attack, he would have to do so against Porter's front, and the Union commander deployed his forces accordingly. On the left, the brigades of Morell's Division of V Corps was stacked up three deep, giving Porter more than enough reserves to protect his flank. The right was covered by Couch's Division of IV Corps, while most of III Corps acted as the right flank reserve. In between these two forces Porter deployed his guns, stretched across the Union front (1). **L & M Batteries of the 3rd US Artillery and A Battery of the 5th US Artillery covered the Union left, while to the right another dozen guns covered the avenues of attack against Couch. The 18 guns on the left and centre were able to cover the ground for a mile to their front, as the terrain was far more open than on any other battlefield of the campaign** (2). **Two slave cabins** (3) **marked the boundary of the guns' line of fire, and the narrow space beyond it was covered by Meagher's Brigade, out in front of Morell. Beyond this lay the cliff. The Confederates tried to bring up artillery to support their attack, but effective counter-battery fire from the Union guns drove these guns back into the cover of the woods. Next came the infantry assaults** (4), **a string of attacks that never came close to piercing the Union centre. A line of skirmishers from Berdan's Sharpshooters** (5) **was strung out in front of the Union line, preventing any Confederate sharp-shooters from picking off the gun crews who were dominating the battlefield. During the afternoon Magruder concentrated his attacks against the Union left, and it was here that the Confederates enjoyed the greatest success of the day. They managed to reach the Union front line, but were driven back by Morell's reserves** (6). **Behind the guns Sumner's II Corps was held in reserve, ready to protect the batteries if they were threatened, but these troops weren't needed, and enjoyed a panoramic view of the battle as it unfolded. As each Confederate attack was repulsed, groups of survivors found slight folds in the ground** (7) **to protect them from the Union shot that was sweeping the battlefield. Many would remain there until darkness covered their retreat. The day ended without any Confederate victory, but thanks to McClellan, Porter was still given orders to abandon his position during the night, and slink away to join his commander at Harrison's Landing. McClellan's lack of enterprise managed to turn a tactical victory into a humiliating strategic defeat. (Stephen Walsh)**

These artillery pieces beside the Watts House mark the location of the guns captured by the 4th Texas Regiment of Hood's Brigade, a scene depicted in a dramatic sketch by Alfred Waud. (Author's Photograph)

37 Union guns ranged against them, many of which were rifled pieces with superior range and accuracy to the majority of the Confederate pieces. A similar fate befell Longstreet's guns on the Confederate right. Only six pieces managed to deploy before Porter's artillery, the siege guns and the naval guns firing in support drove the crews from the plateau. By 4.00pm the Confederate guns had either withdrawn or were silenced. It now fell to the infantry to win the day. What followed was a military blunder on a far greater scale than the "Charge of the Light Brigade" at Balaclava some eight years before, but which was caused by a similar string of misunderstood orders. Lee's plan called for a general attack, spearheaded by Lewis Armistead's Brigade of Huger's Division, the assault to begin when Lee gave the word. The signal for this general assault was to be the advance of Armistead's men, who would let out a Rebel Yell as they moved forward. Somehow the orders that reached Armistead granted him the decision to advance when he saw fit. The most likely author of this misunderstanding was Colonel Robert Chilton, Lee's temporary Chief of Staff, but the truth may never be known. Armistead began his advance, but it stalled under heavy artillery fire, and ground to a halt in a protective dip in the ground in front of two slave cabins. At this moment Magruder arrived well ahead of all but one of his brigades, that of Howell Cobb. After conferring with Lee he moved forward to support Armistead at the head of Cobb's Brigade, as well as two of Huger's formations – the brigades of Mahone and Wright.

The Glendale Crossroads. This important junction needed to be held during 30 June to allow McClellan's supply wagons to pass through. They appeared in the distance on the Darbytown Road, and then headed down the Willis Church Road on the right of the photograph. The road leading off to the left of the junction is the Charles City Road. (Author's Photograph)

Huger was still somewhere to the rear, so Magruder led his ad hoc division forward in person. Charles Weeden watched the assault develop from the Union lines: "*The woods bordering our main field swarmed with gray and butternut coats, and regiments stepped briskly forward, firing as they moved. Our batteries spoke quick and often … Here and there wide rents opened in the ordered files. It never closes, for another gap disorders the men who would try to fill the first … our infantry added their galling fire to the crash of shells … No troops can stand such a fire, and the rebel brigade* [sic] *fell back under cover of the woods after half an hour or more of courageous effort.*" The attack soon faltered then fell apart under withering Union artillery fire, although Mahone and Wright managed to lodge themselves on the extreme left of the Union line, breaking the 14th New York that faced them. For a few minutes it looked as if these troops might turn Porter's flank, but Union reinforcements soon arrived and the momentum was lost. The rest of the advancing Confederate infantry were stopped some 300 yards from the Union line, and after taking further heavy casualties Magruder's line began to fall back. While this was taking place D.H. Hill had deployed in the area where the two roads formed a "V", and he then advanced his brigades in line against the waiting guns of III Corps. As the commander of Rodes' Brigade, Colonel John Gordon was part of the assault: "*My brigade moved across this shell-ploughed plain towards the heights, which were perhaps more than a half mile away. Within 15 or 20 minutes the center regiment, the 3rd Alabama, with which I moved, had left more than half of its number dead and wounded along its track, and the other regiments had suffered almost as severely.*" It was a futile assault, but Gordon found himself in a slight fold in the ground. "*At the foot of the last steep ascent, near the batteries, I found that McClellan's guns were firing over us.*" He ordered his men to lie down, and they remained there, pinned by

TOP **The Union and Confederate lines at Savage's Station ran down the left and right sides of this view respectively. The dip in the middle distance hides the line of the Richmond & York River Railroad, while the site of the station itself is off to the left of the photograph. This view is from the Meadow Road, looking south. (Author's photograph)**

RIGHT **The Trent House served as McClellan's headquarters during late May and most of June 1862, and its location close to Grapevine Bridge meant that the general could easily maintain communications with his Corps commanders on both sides of the Chickahominy River. (Author's photograph)**

Beaver Dam Creek, viewed from its western (or Confederate) bank. The photograph was taken in the area opposite Ellerson's Mill where Dorsey Pender's brigade was halted by concentrated enemy fire. The Union positions were located on top of the ridge seen across the creek, which was only covered in scattered trees in 1862. (Author's photograph)

enemy fire, unable to retreat or advance until darkness came to cover their escape. The assault by Hill, like that of Magruder, was halted or driven back with heavy losses, and the remnants of Hill's brigades who could withdraw retired to the relative safety of the Western Run. The first wave of assaults had failed, and Porter was proving the master of the situation.

Lee decided to order another assault, but this time it had to be more coordinated. The battlefield was becoming too chaotic to achieve this kind of organization, and by this stage Longstreet and Magruder were throwing whole brigades piecemeal into the fray on the Confederate right, which only served to reinforce the failure of the earlier attack. Soon the Confederate side of the battlefield was a sea of stragglers and broken units. The evening was drawing on when Lee managed to launch a final assault. This time the attack would be more coordinated. Magruder and Lafayette McClaws led the ad hoc collection of Confederate units on the western side of the field. D.H. Hill later wrote: *"I never saw anything more grandly heroic than the advance after sunset of the nine brigades under Magruder's orders. Unfortunately they did not move together and were beaten in detail. As each brigade emerged from the woods from 50 to 100 guns opened upon it, tearing great gaps in its ranks, but the heroes reeled on and were shot down by the reserves at the guns, which a few squads reached ... It was not war – it was murder."* Ransom's brigade was one of the shredded units that reached the Union line, only to be driven back by musket fire from Porter's reserves. On the Confederate left, Jackson's Army of the Valley crossed Western Run to launch a valiant assault on Heintzelman's line but, like the assaults that came before, it was halted by heavy fire from III Corps. His men never even reached the place where Gordon's brigade lay trapped in the hollow. Darkness fell, and still the Union guns kept on firing, the blast from their muzzles lighting up the battlefield. Then the slaughter ended. A Union soldier remembered that *"Cheer after cheer went up, shouts of triumph mingled with the peals of cannon ... And closing the terrible tragedy with a halo of inspiration, grand and affecting."*

Lee had lost control of the battle from the start, and consequently his army was led piecemeal into a perfect killing ground to be slaughtered. No amount of dash or bravery could compensate for Porter's massed firepower and that 1/2 mile of deadly space. For his part Porter had little difficulty repulsing the un-coordinated Confederate assaults, and as night fell it was the Confederates who feared what the coming day might bring. Confederate losses had already exceeded 5,500 men killed or wounded on 30 June, as opposed to Porter's losses of 3,200 killed, wounded or missing. Another costly assault might completely break the Army of Northern Virginia. Only Jackson seemed to have grasped what McClellan's next move might be. When his aides tried to wake him during the night, he retorted that, *"McClellan and his army will be gone by daylight,"* and he went back to sleep. He was proved right. When a foggy dawn came, the Confederate scouts who ventured onto the field of slaughter found Malvern Hill empty apart from a small Union rearguard, which fell back as the Confederates advanced. Shortly after the battle ended McClellan had ordered his Corps commanders to resume their retreat. The Union commander viewed Malvern Hill not as a victory, but as a respite from disaster. While many grumbled and even (like Phil Kearny) accused their commanding officer of cowardice or treason, the army had little option but to obey orders and march into the camp at Harrison's Landing. Hundreds of Union warships and transports lay in the river, and supplies were being landed in great piles. As the army arrived in that muddy curve of land it made camp, then details were selected to begin building an extensive series of field fortifications. Harrison's Landing formed a lemon-shaped wedge, bounded to the south by a concave bend of the James River, and to the north by an inlet and the marshy Herring Creek. A spur from the River Road led to the Berkley Plantation near the banks of the river, where McClellan established his headquarters. It was an easily defensible spot, particularly as the James River Flotilla protected every approach.

While Lee's men buried their dead on Malvern Hill, Stuart's cavalry rode in pursuit of McClellan's army. He found them safely ensconced at Harrison's Landing. The Confederates made a demonstration on the northern side of Herring Creek to test the strength of the defenses, but Stuart was soon driven off by fire from the gunboats and a sortie by Smith's Division. At 2.00pm Stuart withdrew, and McClellan was left in peace to improve the defenses of his muddy domain. Stuart duly reported the news to Lee that the Union position was effectively impregnable. By 4 July, Harrison's Landing had been turned into a bastion, and in the words of newsman Joel Cooke the army was now *"fully protected by gunboats and earthworks, and prepared to hold its position against all odds."* The Confederate assault never came. Satisfied that he had driven the enemy from Richmond, Lee decided he could do nothing at Harrison's Landing. Better to pull the army back to Richmond where it could rest and be reequipped. If McClellan ventured out from his earthworks, Lee would be ready for him. McClellan never did, and the campaign came to an end. In a week of almost continual fighting the Confederate Army of Northern Virginia had fought a series of grueling battles, but managed to force their Union opponents to loosen their stranglehold on Richmond, and to retreat back to the safety of their fleet. This was less a victory for the genius of Robert E. Lee and rather the result of the Union commander losing his nerve.

AFTERMATH

The Seven Days Battles lasted only six days, from 26 June until 1 July. However in his written message to his men after the campaign, Lee referred to 2 July being the seventh day, when McClellan fully withdrew behind his defenses at Harrison's Landing, and Lee's rolling series of assaults came to an official end. The name has been used for the campaign ever since. It was during 2 July that Stuart probed McClellan's defenses at Harrison's Landing, and his artillery fired the last shot of the campaign. That morning, McClellan sent a telegram to Stanton that reported: *"I have succeeded in getting the army to this place on the banks of the James River. I have lost but one gun, which had to be abandoned because it broke down. An hour and a half ago the rear of the wagon train was within a mile of the camp, and only one wagon abandoned ... I have not yielded an inch of ground unnecessarily, but have retired to prevent the superior force of the enemy from cutting me off ... and to take a different base of operations."* He continued to pretend that the withdrawal was part of a greater plan, and his line about losing one gun was extremely misleading; the Confederates had already captured over 40 pieces of Union artillery during the week-long campaign. He went on to ask Lincoln for another 100,000 men, which would allow him to "accomplish the great task of capturing Richmond." Lincoln was less willing to accept McClellan's version of events, and was well aware that his army commander had been outmaneuvered and outfought.

On 8 July, Lee ordered his troops to withdraw toward Richmond, where supply dumps had been established to provide the army with fresh food, uniforms and equipment. He was already preparing for a fresh campaign, having dismissed McClellan as a spent force. In fact everyone

The battlefield of Malvern Hill, looking from Magruder's position on the Carter's Mill Road (the lane on the left of the photograph). Porter's guns were deployed a 1/2 mile away across the open field. A slight dip can be seen between the Union and Confederate positions, and this provided some degree of cover for hundreds of Confederate soldiers who were pinned there throughout 1 July. (Author's Photograph)

but McClellan shared the same opinion. Lee took this opportunity to reorganize his army, and to get rid of his least successful commanders. Magruder was sent off to Texas, while Huger and Holmes were also removed from active command. R. H. Anderson was given command of Huger's Division, while Holmes' Division was disbanded and its brigades attached to other formations. McClaws took over the bulk of Magruder's troops, while Jackson was given the benefit of the doubt, and allowed to retain his semi-independent command, at least for the moment. "Stonewall" was well aware that he had performed badly, and he even offered to resign his commission, but Lee refused to accept the resignation. In late June 1862, Lee's objective was to drive McClellan from the gates of Richmond. In his official report to President Davis written within days of the end of the campaign Robert E. Lee stated that: *"Under ordinary circumstances the Federal army should have been destroyed. Its escape was due to ... the want of correct and timely information. This fact, attributable chiefly to the character of the country, enabled General McClellan skillfully to conceal his retreat and to add much to the obstructions with which nature had beset the way of our pursuing columns."* This was partly a smokescreen to protect the reputations of his subordinates, and even of Lee himself. While Lee was able to remove his less reliable subordinates and to create a more efficient headquarters staff, he was left with the knowledge that his army had bungled their one big chance of destroying the enemy, and winning the war by a single feat of arms. However, the public were less concerned with missed opportunities. For them, the matter was simple. A week before, Richmond was under siege, and an enemy army of significantly greater power than the city's defenders lay within earshot of the city's bells. A week later the siege had been lifted, the city had been saved, and the enemy was trapped in a muddy stretch of riverbank, some 30 miles away from Richmond. The man responsible for this miraculous change of events was Robert E. Lee. From that point on the general could do no wrong, and his position as an icon of the Confederacy was assured.

The victory over McClellan meant that Lee could then move the seat of battle north, away from the Confederate capital. After the army finished its reorganization and had recovered its strength, this is exactly what he did. The result was the brilliant campaign fought by Lee and Jackson against Pope's Army of Virginia. During the months that followed, Lee's faith in Jackson would be rewarded by victories at Cedar Mountain (9 August) and at Second Manassas (Bull Run) (29–30 August). The effect of these victories was to open the way for the Confederates' first invasion of the North, a move designed to spare Virginia, and to encourage overseas recognition of the Confederate States of America. However, in July 1862 this lay in the future.

On 11 July, Lincoln appointed General Henry W. Halleck as the new Commander in Chief of the Union army. McClellan read about the appointment in a newspaper. Only days before Stanton and Lincoln had assured McClellan that he still enjoyed their full support. McClellan even began planning for a new offensive, this time on the south side of the James River, along the route that would be taken by Grant two years later. He even wrote to Halleck, stating: *"It is here on the banks of the James that the fate of the Union should be decided."* This was another delusion, and the war had moved on leaving McClellan high and dry on the banks of the James River. Halleck even had to explain the strategic situation to

Kemper's Brigade of Longstreet's Division attacked from right to left across this field during the battle of Frayser's Farm. The photograph was taken looking southward from the Long Bridge Road, toward the site of the Whitlock Farm. The capture of McCall's guns (a scene depicted in the dramatic engraving on Page 60) took place in the left foreground. (Author's photograph)

McClellan, as it was clear "Little Mac" had no longer the desire to grasp the larger strategic picture. Halleck wrote: *"General Pope's Army covering Washington is only 40,000. Your effective force is only about 90,000. You are 30 miles from Richmond, and General Pope 80–90, with the enemy directly between you … In other words, the old Army of the Potomac is split into two parts, and I wish to unite them."* Finally, on 3 August, the order came to embark the remains of the Army of the Potomac, and to transport it to Aquia Creek, south of Washington. After all, McClellan still commanded 90,000 men, who were doing nothing to end the war by sitting in their riverside encampment. Porter and Sumner were duly landed at Aquia Creek during the third week in August, and by the end of the month Sumner had joined forces with General Pope on the Rappahannock River, while Heintzelman was landed at Alexandria, and marched south to join Pope via Manassas. McClellan realized what was afoot, writing to his wife that Stanton would probably *"take the earliest opportunity to relieve me from command and get me out of sight."* He may have taken some comfort from the defeat of his rival, Pope, at Second Manassas, as the result was that McClellan regained control of his army. In fact, as this coincided with Lee's invasion of Maryland, McClellan was able to portray himself as the potential savior of Washington. "Little Mac" would therefore have one last chance to redeem himself. During the Antietam/Sharpsburg campaign that followed, he managed to outmaneuver Lee, but when he had his opponent cornered, with his back to the Potomac River, McClellan proved unable to deliver the knockout blow that could have ended the war. His mismanagement at Antietam was the final straw for Lincoln, who removed McClellan from his command on 7 November 1862. Lincoln then selected Ambrose Burnside as McClellan's replacement, a general whose tenure as commander of the Army of the Potomac proved to be an unmitigated disaster.

The war would continue, and McClellan's Democratic dream of a quick end to the war, or of forcing the Confederacy to the negotiating table and of a mutually agreeable settlement, was shattered by Lee's victory. The campaign would allow Lincoln, Stanton, and the "hawks" of the Republican Party to enforce their definition of victory. From that point on, the war could only be won by the imposition of the Union by brute force, and led to a general hardening of attitudes in the north. The result would be Ulysses S. Grant, William T. Sherman, and the imposition of "total war" and "unconditional surrender". Lee's costly victory during the Seven Days Battles would provide a two-year respite for the Confederate capital, but when the war returned it would do so with a vengeance. The Seven Days Battles had cost the Confederacy 20,614 men, while Union losses amounted to 16,849. Compared to the bloodletting of 1863 and 1864 this was relatively insignificant. However, it was a change that would take the Confederacy down an increasingly bloody road.

ORDERS OF BATTLE

THE ARMY OF THE POTOMAC

– approximately 95,000 men
Commander: Major General George B. McClellan

II Corps

Brigadier General Edwin V. Sumner (17,000 men)

1st Division

Brigadier General Israel B. Richardson

1st Brigade – Brigadier General John C. Caldwell
5th New Hampshire
7th New York
61st New York
91st Pennsylvania

2nd Brigade – Brigadier General Thomas F. Meagher (Colonel Robert Nugent)
29th Massachusetts
63rd New York
69th New York
88th New York

3rd Brigade – Brigadier General William H. French
52nd New York
57th New York
64th New York
66th New York
53rd Pennsylvania
2nd Delaware

Divisional Artillery – Captain George W. Hazzard
1st New York Light Artillery (Battery B) – Captain Rufus D. Petit
4th US Artillery (Batteries A & C) – Captain George W. Hazzard

2nd Division

Brigadier General John Sedgwick

1st Brigade – Colonel Alfred Sully
15th Massachusetts
1st Minnesota
34th New York
82nd New York
Russell's Sharpshooters
Massachusetts Sharpshooters (1 Coy.)

2nd Brigade – Brigadier General William W. Burns
69th Pennsylvania
71st Pennsylvania
72nd Pennsylvania
106th Pennsylvania

3rd Brigade – Brigadier General Napoleon J.T. Dana
19th Massachusetts
20th Massachusetts
7th Michigan
42nd New York

Divisional Artillery – Colonel Charles H. Tomkins
1st Rhode Island Light Artillery (Battery A) – Captain John A. Tompkins
1st US Artillery (Battery I) – Lieutenant Edmund Kelly

Corps Artillery Reserve
1st New York Light Artillery (Battery G) – Captain John D. Frank
1st Rhode Island Light Artillery (Battery B) – Captain Walter O. Bartlett
1st Rhode Island Light Artillery (Battery G) – Captain Charles D. Owen

Corps Cavalry
6th New York Cavalry (4 Coys., D, F, H, K)

III Corps

Brigadier General Samuel P. Heintzelman (17,500 men)

2nd Division

Brigadier General Joseph Hooker

1st Brigade – Brigadier General Cuvier Grover
1st Massachusetts
11th Massachusetts
16th Massachusetts
2nd New Hampshire
26th Pennsylvania

2nd Brigade – Brigadier General Daniel E. Sickles
70th New York
71st New York
72nd New York
73rd New York
74th New York

3rd Brigade – Brigadier General Joseph P. Carr
5th New Jersey
6th New Jersey
7th New Jersey
8th New Jersey
2nd New York

Divisional Artillery – Lieutenant Colonel Charles S. Wainwright
1st New York Light (Battery D) – Captain Thomas W. Osborn
4th New York Light – Lieutenant Joseph Nairn
1st US Artillery (Battery H) – Captain Charles H. Webber

3rd Division

Brigadier General Philip Kearny

1st Brigade – Brigadier General John C. Robinson
20th Indiana
87th New York
57th Pennsylvania
63rd Pennsylvania
105th New York

2nd Brigade – Brigadier General David B. Birney
3rd Maine
4th Maine
38th New York
40th New York
101st New York

3rd Brigade – Brigadier General Hiram G. Berry
2nd Michigan
3rd Michigan
5th Michigan
1st New York
37th New York

Divisional Artillery – Captain James Thompson
1st Rhode Island Light (Battery E) – Captain George E. Randolph
2nd US Artillery (Battery G) – Captain James Thompson

Corps Artillery Reserve – Captain Gustavus A. DeRussy
6th New York Light – Captain Walter P. Bramhall
2nd New Jersey Light – Captain John E. Beam
4th US Artillery (Battery K) – DeRussy, Lieutenant Francis W. Seeley

Corps Cavalry – Colonel William W. Averell
3rd Pennsylvania Cavalry

IV Corps

Brigadier General Erasmus S. Keyes (8,000 men)

1st Division

Brigadier General Darius N. Couch

1st Brigade – Brigadier General Albion P. Howe
55th New York
62nd New York
93rd Pennsylvania
98th New York
102nd Pennsylvania

2nd Brigade – Brigadier General John J. Abercrombie
65th New York
67th New York
23rd Pennsylvania
31st Pennsylvania
61st Pennsylvania

3rd Brigade – Brigadier General Innis N. Palmer
7th Massachusetts
10th Massachusetts
36th New York
2nd Rhode Island

Divisional Artillery
1st Pennsylvania Light Artillery (Battery C) – Captain Jeremiah McCarthy
1st Pennsylvania Light Artillery (Battery D) – Captain Edward H. Flood

Divisional Cavalry
6th New York Cavalry (Coy F)

2nd Division

Brigadier General John J. Peck

1st Brigade – Brigadier General Henry M. Naglee
11th Maine
56th New York
100th New York
52nd Pennsylvania
104th Pennsylvania

2nd Brigade – Brigadier General Henry W. Wessells
81st New York
85th New York
92nd New York
96th New York
98th New York
85th Pennsylvania
101st Pennsylvania
103rd Pennsylvania

Divisional Artillery – Captain Peter C. Regan
1st New York Light Artillery (Battery H) – Lieutenant Charles E. Minck
7th New York Light Artillery – Captain Peter C. Regan

Divisional Cavalry
6th New York Cavalry (Coy H)

Corps Artillery Reserve – Major Robert M. West
8th New York Light Artillery – Captain Butler Fitch
1st Pennsylvania Light Artillery (Battery E) – Captain Theodore Miller
1st Pennsylvania Light Artillery (Battery H) – Captain James Brady
5th US Artillery (Battery M) – Captain James McKnight

Corps Cavalry – Colonel David McM. Gregg
8th Pennsylvania Cavalry

V Corps

Brigadier General Fitz-John Porter (25,000 men)

1st Division

Brigadier General George W. Morell

1st Brigade – Brigadier General John H. Martindale
2nd Maine
18th Massachusetts (attached to Stoneman's Cavalry during campaign)
22nd Massachusetts
1st Michigan
13th New York
25th New York
Massachusetts Sharpshooters (1 Coy.)

2nd Brigade – Brigadier General Charles Griffin
9th Massachusetts
4th Michigan
14th New York
62nd Pennsylvania

3rd Brigade – Brigadier General Daniel Butterfield
12th New York
17th New York (attached to Stoneman's Cavalry during campaign)
44th New York
16th Michigan
83rd Pennsylvania
Michigan Sharpshooters (1 Coy.)

Divisional Artillery – Captain William B. Weeden
Massachusetts Light Artillery (3rd, Battery C) – Captain Augustus P. Martin
Massachusetts Light Artillery (5th, Battery E) – Lieutenant John B. Hyde
1st Rhode Island Light Artillery (Battery C) – Captain William B. Weeden
5th US Artillery (Battery D) – Lieutenant Henry W. Kingsbury

Attached Sharpshooters – Colonel Hiram Berdan
1st US Sharpshooters

2nd Division
Brigadier General George Sykes

1st Brigade – Brigadier General Robert C. Buchanan
3rd US
4th US
12th US
14th US

2nd Brigade – Lieutenant Colonel William Chapman (Major Charles S. Lovell)
2nd US
6th US
10th US
11th US
17th US

3rd Brigade – Colonel Gouverneur K. Warren
5th New York
10th New York

Divisional Artillery – Captain Stephen H. Weed
3rd US Artillery (Batteries L & M)
5th US Artillery (Battery I)

3rd Division (Pennsylvania Reserves)
Brigadier General George A. McCall (Brigadier General Truman Seymour)

1st Brigade – Brigadier General John F. Reynolds (Colonel Senecca G. Simmons, Colonel R. Biddle Roberts)
1st Pennsylvania Reserves
2nd Pennsylvania Reserves
5th Pennsylvania Reserves
8th Pennsylvania Reserves
13th Pennsylvania Reserves

2nd Brigade – Brigadier General George W. Meade (Colonel Albert L. Magilton)
3rd Pennsylvania Reserves
4th Pennsylvania Reserves
7th Pennsylvania Reserves
11th Pennsylvania Reserves

3rd Brigade – Brigadier General Truman Seymour (Colonel C. Feger Jackson)
6th Pennsylvania Reserves (attached to White House Garrison during campaign)
9th Pennsylvania Reserves
10th Pennsylvania Reserves
12th Pennsylvania Reserves

Divisional Artillery – Captain Henry V. De Hart
1st Pennsylvania Light Artillery (Battery A) – Captain Hezekiah Easton
1st Pennsylvania Light Artillery (Battery B) – Captain James H. Cooper
1st Pennsylvania Light Artillery (Battery G) – Captain Mark Kerns
5th US Artillery (Battery C) – Captain Henry V. De Hart

Cavalry – Colonel James H. Childs
4th Pennsylvania Cavalry (6 Coys)

Corps Cavalry – Colonel. John F. Farnsworth
8th Illinois Cavalry

Corps Artillery Reserve – Colonel Henry J. Hunt
1st Artillery Brigade – Lieutenant Colonel William Hays
2nd US Artillery (Battery A) – Captain John C. Tidball
2nd US Artillery (Batteries B & L) – Captain James M. Robertson
2nd US Artillery (Battery M) – Captain Henry Benson
3rd US Artillery (Batteries C & G) – Captain Horatio Gibson (attached to White House Garrison during campaign)

2nd Artillery Brigade – Lieutenant Colonel George W. Getty
1st US Artillery (Battery E) – Lieutenant Alanson L. Randol
1st US Artillery (Battery G)
1st US Artillery (Battery K) – Lieutenant Samuel S. Elder
4th US Artillery (Battery G) – Lieutenant Charles H. Morgan
5th US Artillery (Battery A) – Lieutenant Adalbert Ames
5th US Artillery (Battery K) – Captain John R. Smead

3rd Artillery Brigade – Major Albert Arndt
1st Battalion, New York Light Artillery (Battery A) – Captain Otto Diederichs
1st Battalion, New York Light Artillery (Battery B) – Captain Adolph Voegelee
1st Battalion, New York Light Artillery (Battery C) – Captain John Knieriem
1st Battalion, New York Light Artillery (Battery D) – Captain Grimm

4th Artillery Brigade – Major E.R. Petheridge
Maryland Light Artillery (Battery A) – Captain John W. Wolcott
Maryland Light Artillery (Battery B) – Captain Alonzo Snow

5th Artillery Brigade – Captain J. Howard Carlisle
2nd US Artillery (Battery E) – Captain J. Howard Carlisle
3rd US Artillery (Batteries F & K) – Captain La Rhett L. Livingston

Siege Train
1st Connecticut Heavy Artillery – Captain Robert O. Tyler

VI Corps
Brigadier General William B. Franklin (17,000 men)

1st Division
Brigadier General Henry W. Slocum

1st Brigade – Brigadier General George W. Taylor
1st New Jersey
2nd New Jersey
3rd New Jersey
4th New Jersey

2nd Brigade – Brigadier General Joseph J. Bartlett
5th Maine
16th New York
27th New York
96th Pennsylvania

3rd Brigade – Brigadier General John Newton
18th New York
31st New York
32nd New York
95th Pennsylvania

Divisional Artillery – Captain Edward R. Platt
Massachusetts Light Artillery (1st Battery A) – Captain Edward R. Platt
1st New Jersey Light Artillery – Captain William Hexamer
2nd US Artillery (Battery D) – Lieutenant Emory Upton

2nd Division
Brigadier General William F. Smith

1st Brigade – Brigadier General Winfield S. Hancock
6th Maine
43rd New York
49th Pennsylvania
5th Wisconsin

2nd Brigade – Brigadier General W.T.H. Brooks
2nd Vermont
3rd Vermont
4th Vermont
5th Vermont
6th Vermont

3rd Brigade – Brigadier General John W. Davidson
7th Maine
20th New York
33rd New York
49th New York
77th New York

Divisional Artillery – Captain Romeyn B. Ayres
1st New York Light Artillery (Battery E) – Captain Charles C. Wheeler
1st New York Light Artillery – Lieutenant Andrew Cowan
3rd New York Light Artillery – Captain Thaddeus P. Mott
5th US Artillery (Battery F) – Captain Romeyn B. Ayres

Attached Cavalry
5th Pennsylvania Cavalry (2 Coys, I & K)

Corps Cavalry
1st New York

Army Cavalry Reserve
Brigadier General Philip St George Cooke (5,500 men)

1st Cavalry Brigade – Brigadier General William H. Emory
6th Pennsylvania Cavalry
5th US Cavalry (5 Coys., A, D, E, H & I)

2nd Cavalry Brigade – Colonel George A.H. Blake
1st US Cavalry (4 Coys., A, C, F & H)
4th Pennsylvania Cavalry (4 Coys.)

Advance Guard– Brigadier General George Stoneman
6th US Cavalry
17th New York Cavalry
18th Massachusetts Cavalry
5th US Cavalry (5 Coys., B, C, F, G & J)
3rd US Artillery (Batteries C, D, E, F & G)

White House Garrison – Brigadier General Silas Casey (4,500 men)
11th Pennsylvanian Cavalry (5 Coys., B, D, F, I & K)
93rd New York (6 Coys., B, C, D, E, G & I)
1st New York Light Artillery (Battery F) – Captain William R. Wilson

Engineers (Volunteer Engineer Brigade) – Brigadier General Daniel P. Woodbury
15th New York Engineers
50th New York Engineers
US Engineer Battalion (3 Coys., A, B & C) – Captain James C. Duane

Army Headquarters Guard
2nd US Cavalry
4th US Cavalry (2 Coys., A & E)
Oneida (New York) Cavalry
McClellan Dragoons (Illinois)
8th US Infantry (2 Coys., F & G)
93rd New York (4 Coys., A, F, H & K)
Sturgis Rifles (Illinois)

THE ARMY OF NORTHERN VIRGINIA
approximately 85,000 men
Commander: General Robert E. Lee

The Richmond Divisions

Major General Ambrose P. Hill's "Light" Division
(14,000 men)

Brigadier General Charles W. Field's Brigade
40th Virginia
47th Virginia
55th Virginia
60th Virginia

Brigadier General Maxcy Gregg's Brigade
1st South Carolina
12th South Carolina
13th South Carolina
14th South Carolina
1st South Carolina Rifles

Brigadier General Joseph R. Anderson's Brigade (Col Edward L. Thomas)
14th Georgia
35th Georgia
35th Georgia
49th Georgia
3rd Louisiana (battalion)

Brigadier General Lawrence O'B. Branch's Brigade
7th North Carolina
18th North Carolina
28th North Carolina
33rd North Carolina
37th North Carolina

Brigadier General James J. Archer's Brigade
5th Alabama (battalion)
19th Georgia
1st Tennessee
7th Tennessee
14th Tennessee

Brigadier General William D. Pender's Brigade
2nd Arkansas (battalion)
16th North Carolina
22nd North Carolina
34th North Carolina
38th North Carolina
22nd Virginia (battalion)

Divisional Artillery
1st Maryland Artillery Battery – Captain R. Snowden Andrews
Charleston German Artillery Battery (South Carolina) – Captain William K. Bachman
Fredericksburg Artillery Battery (Virginia) – Captain Carter M. Braxton
Captain William G. Crenshaw's Artillery Battery (Virginia)
Letcher Artillery Battery (Virginia) – Captain Greenlee Davidson
Captain Marmaduke Johnston's Artillery Battery (Virginia)
Captain L. Masters' Artillery Battery (Virginia)
Pee Dee Artillery Battery (South Carolina) – Captain David G. McIntosh
Purcell Artillery Battery (Virginia) – Captain William J. Pegram

Major General Daniel H. Hill's Division
(10,000 men)

Brigadier General Robert E. Rodes' Brigade (Colonel John B. Gordon)
3rd Alabama
5th Alabama
6th Alabama
12th Alabama
26th Alabama

Brigadier General Samuel Garland Jr.'s Brigade
5th North Carolina
12th North Carolina
13th North Carolina
20th North Carolina
23rd North Carolina

Brigadier General George B. Anderson's Brigade (Colonel C.C. Tew)
2nd North Carolina
4th North Carolina
14th North Carolina
30th North Carolina

Colonel Alfred H. Colquitt's Brigade
13th Alabama

6th Georgia
23rd Georgia
27th Georgia
28th Georgia

Brigadier General Roswell S. Ripley's Brigade
44th Georgia
48th Georgia
1st North Carolina
3rd North Carolina

Divisional Artillery
Jeff Davis Artillery Battery (Alabama) – Captain J.W. Bondurant
King William Artillery Battery (Virginia) – Captain Thomas H. Carter
Long Island Artillery Battery (Virginia) – Captain P.H. Clark (temporarily attached)
Captain R.A. Hardaway's Artillery Battery (Alabama)
Hanover Artillery Battery (Virginia) – Captain George W. Nelson
Richmond Orange (Artillery Battery (Virginia) – Lieutenant. C.W. Fry (temporarily attached)
Captain A. Burnet Rhett's Artillery Battery (South Carolina) (temporarily attached)

Major General James Longstreet's Division[3]
(9,000 men)

Colonel James L. Kemper's Brigade
1st Virginia
7th Virginia
11th Virginia
17th Virginia
24th Virginia
Loudon Artillery Battery (Virginia) – Captain Arthur L. Rogers

Brigadier General Robert H. Anderson's Brigade[4]
2nd South Carolina Rifles
4th South Carolina
5th South Carolina
6th South Carolina
Palmetto Sharpshooters (South Carolina)

Brigadier General George E. Pickett's Brigade (Colonel Eppa Hunton, Colonel John B. Strange)
8th Virginia
18th Virginia
19th Virginia
28th Virginia
56th Virginia

Brigadier General Cadmus M. Wilcox's Brigade
8th Alabama
9th Alabama
10th Alabama
11th Alabama
Thomas Artillery Battery (Virginia) – Captain Edwin J. Anderson

Brigadier General Roger A. Pryor's Brigade
14th Alabama
14th Louisiana
2nd Florida
1st Louisiana Zouave (battalion)/St Paul's Foot Rifles (Louisiana)
3rd Virginia
Donaldsonville Artillery Battery (Louisiana) – Captain Victor Maurin

Brigadier General Winfield S. Featherston's Brigade
12th Mississippi
19th Mississippi
2nd Mississippi (battalion)
Richmond Howitzers (3rd Co.) (Virginia) – Captain Benjamin H. Smith Jr.

Divisional Artillery
Washington Artillery (1st Co.) (Louisiana) – Captain Charles W. Squires
Washington Artillery (2nd Co.) (Louisiana) – Captain John B. Richardson
Washington Artillery (3rd Co.) (Louisiana) – Captain M.B. Miller
Washington Artillery (4th Co.) (Louisiana) – Captain Joseph Norcom
Lynchburg Artillery Battery (Virginia) – Captain James Dearing
Dixie Artillery Battery (Virginia) – Captain William H. Chapman

The Valley Army
Major General Thomas L. Jackson

Army Assets
2nd Virginia Cavalry

Brigadier General William H.C. Whiting's Division
(4,000 men) (temporarily attached)

Colonel Evander McIver Law's Brigade
4th Alabama
2nd Mississippi
11th Mississippi
6th North Carolina

Brigadier General John B. Hood's Brigade
18th Georgia
1st Texas
4th Texas
5th Texas
Hampton's Legion (South Carolina)

Divisional Artillery
Staunton Artillery Battery (Virginia) – Captain William L. Blathis
Rowan Artillery Battery (North Carolina) – Captain James Reilly

Major General Thomas L. Jackson's Division[5]
[7,500 men]

Brigadier General Charles S. Winder's Brigade "The Stonewall Brigade"
2nd Virginia
4th Virginia
5th Virginia
27th Virginia
33rd Virginia
Allegheny Artillery Battery (Virginia) – Lieutenant John C. Carpenter
Rockbridge Artillery Battery (Virginia) – Captain William T. Poague

Brigadier General John R. Jones' Brigade (Lieutenant Colonel R.H. Cunningham Jr.)
21st Virginia
42nd Virginia
48th Virginia
1st Virginia "Irish" (battalion)
Richmond Hampden Artillery Battery (Virginia) – Captain William H. Haskie

Colonel E.V. Fulkerson's Brigade (E.T.H. Warren, Brigadier General Wade Hampton)
10th Virginia
23rd Virginia
37th Virginia
Danville Artillery Battery (Virginia) – Captain George W. Wooding

Brigadier General Alexander R. Lawton's Brigade
13th Georgia
26th Georgia
31st Georgia
38th Georgia
60th Georgia (4th battalion)
61st Georgia

Divisional Artillery
Jackson Artillery Battery (Virginia) – Captain W.E. Cutshaw

Major General Richard Ewell's Division
(6,500 men)

Brigadier General Arnold Elzey's Brigade (Colonel James A. Walker, Brigadier General Jubal Early)
12th Georgia
13th Virginia
25th Virginia
31st Virginia
44th Virginia
52nd Virginia
58th Virginia

Brigadier General Isaac R. Trimble's Brigade
15th Alabama
21st Georgia
16th Mississippi
21st North Carolina
1st North Carolina (battalion)
Henrico Artillery Battery (Virginia) – Captain. A.R. Courtney

Brigadier General Richard Taylor's Brigade (Colonel I.G. Seymour, Colonel Leroy A. Stafford)
6th Louisiana
7th Louisiana
8th Louisiana
9th Louisiana ("Louisiana Tigers")
Charlottesville Artillery Battery (Virginia) – Captain J. Carrington

Colonel Bradley T. Johnson's Maryland Line (Demi-Brigade)
1st Maryland
Baltimore Artillery Battery (Maryland) – Captain J.B. Brockenborough

Magruder's Command
Major General John B. Magruder (13,000 men)

Brigadier General David R. Jones' Division

Brigadier General Robert Toombs' Brigade
2nd Georgia
15th Georgia
17th Georgia
20th Georgia

Colonel George T. Anderson's Brigade
1st Georgia Regulars
7th Georgia
8th Georgia
9th Georgia
11th Georgia

Divisional Artillery
Wise Artillery Battery (Virginia) – Captain James S. Brown
Washington Artillery Battery (South Carolina) – Captain James F. Hart
Sumter Artillery (Co. E) (Georgia) – Captain John Lane (temporarily attached)
Madison Artillery Battery (Louisiana) – Captain George F. Moody
Ashland Artillery Battery (Virginia) - Lieutenant James Woolfolk
Captain W.J. Dabney's Artillery Battery (Virginia)

Brigadier General Lafayette McLaws' Division

Brigadier General Paul J. Semmes' Brigade
10th Georgia
53rd Georgia
5th Louisiana
10th Louisiana
15th Virginia
32nd Virginia
Captain Basil C. Manly's Artillery Battery (North Carolina)

Brigadier General Joseph B. Kershaw's Brigade
2nd South Carolina
3rd South Carolina
7th South Carolina
8th South Carolina
Alexandria Artillery Battery (Virginia) – Captain Del Kemper

Major General John B. Magruder's Division
(commanded directly by Magruder himself)

Brigadier General Richard Griffith's Brigade (Colonel William Barksdale)
13th Mississippi
17th Mississippi
18th Mississippi
21st Mississippi
Richmond Howitzers (1st Co.) (Virginia) – Captain E.S. McCarthy

Brigadier General Howell Cobb's Brigade
16th Georgia
24th Georgia
2nd Louisiana
15th North Carolina
Cobb's Legion (Georgia)
Troup Artillery Battery (Georgia) – Captain Henry H. Carlton

Divisional Artillery – Colonel Stephen D. Lee
Amherst Artillery Battery (Virginia) – Captain Thomas J. Kirkpatrick (temporarily attached)
Magruder Artillery Battery (Virginia) – Captain T. Jeff Page Jr.
Pulaski Artillery Battery (Georgia) – Captain J.P.W. Read
James City Artillery Battery (Virginia) – Captain L.W. Richardson

Brigadier General Benjamin Huger's Division
(8,000 men) (temporarily attached)

Brigadier General Lewis A. Armistead's Brigade
9th Virginia
14th Virginia
38th Virginia
53rd Virginia
57th Virginia (part of regiment in Walker's Brigade)
5th Virginia (battalion)
Fauquier Artillery Battery (Virginia) – Captain Robert M. Stribling
Goochland Artillery Battery (Virginia) – Captain William H Turner

Brigadier General William Mahone's Brigade
6th Virginia
12th Virginia
16th Virginia
41st Virginia
49th Virginia
Portsmouth Artillery Battery (Virginia) – Captain Carey F. Grimes
Lynchburg Beauregard Artillery Battery (Virginia) – Captain M.N. Moorman

Brigadier General Ambrose R. Wright's Brigade
3rd Georgia
4th Georgia
22nd Georgia
44th Alabama
1st Louisiana
Virginia Light Artillery (Co. D) – Captain Frank Huger
Sumter Artillery (Co. D) (Georgia) – Captain H.M. Ross (temporarily attached)

Major General Theophilus H. Holmes' Division[6]
(6,500 men)

Brigadier General Robert Ranson Jr.'s Brigade
24th North Carolina
25th North Carolina
26th North Carolina
35th North Carolina
48th North Carolina (detached 29 June–1 July)
49th North Carolina

Brigadier General Junius Daniel's Brigade
43rd North Carolina
45th North Carolina
50th North Carolina
14th Virginia Cavalry Battalion

Brigadier General John G. Walker's Brigade (Colonel Van H. Manning)
3rd Arkansas
2nd Georgia (battalion)
27th North Carolina
46th North Carolina
48th North Carolina (attached 29 June–1 July)
30th Virginia
57th Virginia (part of regiment in Armistead's Brigade)
Petersburg Cavalry (Virginia)

Brigadier General Henry A. Wise's Brigade (attached)
26th Virginia
46th Virginia
4th Virginia Heavy Artillery (Infantry)
10th Virginia Cavalry (attached to Stuart's Cavalry Command)
Captain W.C. Andrews' Artillery Battery (Alabama)
Captain A.D. Armistead's Artillery Battery (Virginia)
Captain D.A. French's Artillery Battery (Virginia)
Nelson Artillery Battery (Virginia) – Captain J.H. Rives

Divisional Artillery
Captain James R. Branch's Artillery Battery (Virginia)
Captain T.H. Brems' Artillery Battery (North Carolina)
Captain Thomas B. French's Artillery Battery (Virginia)
Captain Edward Graham's Artillery Battery (Virginia)
Captain Charles R. Grandy's Artillery Battery (Virginia)
Captain W.P. Lloyd's Artillery Battery (North Carolina)

Army Assets

Artillery Reserve
Brigadier General William N. Pendleton

1st Virginia Artillery Battalion – Colonel J. Thompson Brown
Williamsburg Artillery Battery (Virginia) – Captain John A. Coke
Richmond Fayette Artillery Battery (Virginia) – Lieutenant William I. Clopton
Richmond Howitzers (Virginia), (2nd Coy.) – Captain David Watson

Jones' Artillery Battalion – Major H.P. Jones
Long Island Artillery Battery (Virginia) – Captain P.H. Clark
Orange Richmond Artillery Battery (Virginia) – Lieutenant C.W. Fry
Captain A. Burnet Rhett's Artillery Battery (South Carolina)

Nelson's Artillery Battalion – Major William Nelson
Fluvanna Artillery Battery (Virginia) – Captain Charles T. Tuckstep
Amherst Artillery Battery (Virginia) – Captain Thomas J. Kirkpatrick
Morris Artillery Battery (Virginia) – Captain R.C.M. Page

Richardson's Artillery Battalion – Major Charles Richardson
2nd Fluvanna Artillery Battery (Virginia) – Captain John C. Ancell
Captain John Milledge's Artillery Battery (Georgia)
Ashland Artillery Battery (Virginia) – Lieutenant James Woolfolk

Sumner Artillery Battalion (Georgia) – Lieutenant Colonel A.S. Cutts
Sumner Battalion (Coy. A) – Captain H.M. Ross
Sumner Battalion (Coy B) – Captain John Price
Sumner Battalion (Coy. D) – Captain James Ap Blackshear
Sumner Battalion (Coy E) – Captain John Vane
Captain S.P. Hamilton's Artillery Battery (Georgia)

Cavalry Reserve
Brigadier General J.E.B. Stuart (3,000 men)
1st Virginia Cavalry
3rd Virginia Cavalry
4th Virginia Cavalry
5th Virginia Cavalry
9th Virginia Cavalry
10th Virginia Cavalry
1st North Carolina Cavalry
15th Virginia Cavalry Battalion
Cobb's Legion Cavalry (Georgia)
Jeff Davis Legion Cavalry (Mississippi)
Hampton's Legion Cavalry (South Carolina)
Wise's Legion (Virginia)
Captain John Pelham's Horse Artillery Battery (Virginia)
Captain R. Preston Chew's Horse Artillery Battery (Virginia)

3 Effectively commanded by Brigadier General Robert H. Anderson, as Longstreet also acted as an ad-hoc Corps commander during the campaign.
4 Commanded by Colonel Micah Jenkins when Anderson commanded the Division.
5 Effectively commanded by Brigadier General Charles S. Winder during the campaign
6 Attached to Army of Northern Virginia, this was an independent division detached from the Department of North Carolina.

THE BATTLEFIELD TODAY

While much of the ground covered by the warring armies in June 1862 is buried in a sprawl of commuting homes and farmland, enough survives to give the visitor an appreciation of the terrain over which the campaign was fought, and even the roads over which the troops marched. In July 1944, Congress established the Richmond National Battlefield Park, based on ground bought by a group of Virginians whose aim was to preserve their military heritage. Their purchases were donated to the Commonwealth of Virginia in 1932, and after the establishment of the Battlefield Park more land was added, creating a string of sites that allow visitors to trace the course of the campaign. It also covers the battles that were fought over the same ground by Lee and Grant in 1864. Today the Richmond National Battlefield Park is administered by the National Park Service.

The starting point of any tour is naturally Richmond, where the National Park Service maintains a superb museum, audio-visual interpretation center and well-stocked bookstore in its Richmond headquarters, located in the building of what was once the Tredegar Ironworks on the banks of the James River. Although difficult to find due to poor street signage, the center is an essential part of any battlefield tour, and the NPS provide touring guides to their battlefield sites. Their complete tour involves a 57-mile circuit that loops around both banks of the Chickahominy River, and then returns to Richmond via the River Road. It encompasses sites relevant to both the 1862 and 1864 campaigns, as well as important secondary sites such as Drewry's Bluff, the Chimborazo Park (the site of the great Confederate hospital), and Forts Brady and Harrison, part of Richmond's late-war river defenses.

Taking Route 360 north from the city center, the first stop is at Chickahominy Bluff, the vantage point from which Lee watched the fighting around Mechanicsville on the far side of the Chickahominy River. Today Lee would find his view obscured by trees, but interpretative plaques provide visitors with an understanding of what could be seen in 1862. After crossing the Chickahominy visitors are directed to turn east at Mechanicsville onto State Road 156. Much of the battlefield here has been lost to development, and an interstate highway (I-295) now cuts through the area where McCall's troops held the bridge over the creek. However, the Richmond National Battlefield Park contains a parcel of land surrounding the site of Ellerson's Mill (since demolished), and the site of the attack by Ripley, and Pender's Brigades. Visitors can gain some idea of the swampy nature of the creek, and the scale of the bluff behind it.

Continuing east along State Road 156 past the site of Walnut Grove Church and then Gaine's Mill and the crossing over Powhite Creek, visitors are directed to turn off south toward the Gaine's Mill unit of the

Battlefield Park. This is somewhat more rewarding as a substantial portion of this complicated battlefield was saved from development. The area around the Watts house has been preserved, and a series of trails allow visitors to follow the course of the battle as they wind down to Boatswain's Creek, then climb the bluff back toward the Watts House. Markers provide a high level of interpretation, and show where all the key events took place in the center and on the left of the Union line. Secondary trails lead around the left flank of the Union line, where Longstreet made his attacks. Returning to the main road, visitors can drive past the Cold Harbor portion of the Battlefield Park, where Lee held Grant in 1864. From Cold Harbor the Battlefield Trail leads south on the Cold Harbor Road to the site of Grapevine Bridge, where visitors can gain a good impression of the size of the Chickahominy River. The trail turns left onto Grapevine Road immediately after the crossing to avoid I-295, and in so doing it passes the Trent House, where McClellan established his headquarters during 26 and 27 June 1862. The official trail continues on to the Fair Oaks and Seven Pines area, but by continuing on to the south then east along Meadow Road you reach the site of Savage's Station. Unfortunately two interstates cross on top of the battlefield (I-295 and I-64), but by following Meadow Road to the east visitors can look south across the railroad line toward the site of the clash between Kershaw and Burns. The more ambitious can even follow a lane to the site of Savage's Station, although this area is about to be developed. Virginia Civil War Trails markers and Virginia Historical Markers provide some degree of interpretation here. Incidentally the signage and interpretative markers provided by these two groups are of the highest order, and can be found at regular intervals as you tour the battlefields. After crossing under I-64 Meadow Road turns into State Road 156, and leads south to the White Oak Swamp Bridge.

Although houses now cover the site of Jackson's artillery line (along what is now Portugee Road), the area from his deployment area near Union Church south to the bridge is largely undeveloped and marshy. The White Oak Swamp is a designated wetland, and therefore cannot be developed. Markers at the site of the bridge explain what happened there on 30 June 1862. On the south side of the bridge the Union lines can be traced immediately before the junction of Road 156 and Hines Road. Continuing on down State Road 156 (now the Darbytown Road) you reach the Glendale Crossroads, almost as undeveloped now as it was then. The whole area of the battlefield is covered in arable land, woodland, and small farms, similar to 1862. This makes Frayser's Farm one of the more rewarding battlefields to visit, partly because the lack of signage means you have to provide your own interpretation. This said, a group of markers is found at the crossroads, and another is located on the junction of the Darbytown Road and Long Bridge Road, along which Longstreet made his assault on 30 June 1862. A good feel for this part of the battlefield can be gained amongst the woods and cornfields south and east of the road. Kearny's Division held a line immediately south of the Charles City Road, and the spot where Hines Road joins this road from the west marks the corner of the Union line, where Slocum faced off Huger. Returning to the crossroads, State Road 156 becomes the Willis Church Road, and leads to the Glendale National Cemetery. The Battlefield Park maintains a small unit close to the site of Frayser's

Farm, while a lane running west from the main road leads to land bought by the Civil War Preservation Trust (CWPT), marking the site where Burns' Brigade clashed with Branch. Willis Church can be found a few yards down the main road, and again the CWPT have bought a parcel of land in the area close to the Willis Church Parsonage where Jackson's men deployed. The remains of the Parsonage can still be seen, and stand close to the spot were Lee established his headquarters during the battle of Malvern Hill. The Battlefield Park owns an extensive piece of land on Malvern Hill (over 500 acres), allowing the visitor to understand the topography of the area. It is surprising how flat the hill appears from the Confederate side, but on closer inspection the small folds in the ground that provided the attackers with some cover can be seen in the centre of the plateau. A network of trails and markers allows visitors to walk along the Union gun line on Porter's side of the field, and then continue on to the Crew House, where they can inspect the Malvern Hill Cliffs. Another line of guns 1/2 mile to the north marks the spot where Longstreet tried to establish his grand battery. Walking that deadly space between the two gun lines is a sobering experience.

To finish the tour, trace the route of the Army of the Potomac's retreat along the Carter's Mill Road (County Road 606) until it joins the River Road (now Route 5). It leads east then south past the Shirley Plantation toward the Berkley Plantation, at Harrison's Landing. Although the area is in private hands, the house and grounds are open to visitors, and provide a good view of the James River. After completing this tour of the battlefields, you can return to Richmond by driving back along Route 5.

BIBLIOGRAPHY

Allan, William, *The Army of Northern Virginia in 1862* (Dayton, OH, 1984) Morningside Press, originally published1892
Battle, Jesse Sumner, & Adams, James Norman, *Civil War Letters* (Cleveland, OH, 1979) Halle Park Press
Bowers, John, *Stonewall Jackson: Portrait of a Soldier* (New York, NY, 1989) Morrow Press
Bridges, Hal, *Lee's Maverick General: Daniel Harvey Hill* (New York, NY, 1961) McGraw-Hill
Burton, Brian K., *Extraordinary Circumstances: The Seven Days Battles* (Bloomington, IN, 2001) Indiana University Press
Casdorph, Paul D., *Lee and Jackson: Confederate Chieftains* (New York, NY, 1992) Aragon House
Casdorph, Paul D., *Prince John Magruder: His Life and Campaigns* (New York, NY, 1996) John Wiley & Sons
Catton, Bruce, *Mr. Lincoln's Army* (New York, NY, 1962) Doubleday
Cullen, Joseph P., *Richmond Battlefields: A History and Guide to the Richmond Battlefield Park* (Washington, DC, 1961) National Park Service
Cullen, Joseph P., *The Peninsula Campaign, 1862: McClellan and Lee struggle for Richmond* (New York, NY, 1973) Bonanza Publishing
Dowdey, Clifford, *Lee takes Command* (New York, NY, 1964) Barnes & Noble
Dowdey, Clifford, *The Seven Days: The Emergence of Robert E. Lee* (Wilmington, NC, 1988) Broadfoot
Eckenrode, H.J., & Conrad, Bryan, *George B. McClellan: The man who saved the Union* (Chapel Hill, NC, 1941) University of North Carolina Press
Esposito, Vincent (ed.), *The West Point Atlas of American Wars* (New York, NY, 1995) Henry Holt & Co. First published 1959. Vol. 1 (1689–1900)
Jonson, Robert U., & Buel, Clarence C. (eds.), *Battles and Leaders of the Civil War* (New York, NY, 1887) Century Company. Four volumes. Reprinted by Castle Press (Edison, NJ, 1987). Note that this source contains articles originally published in *Century* Magazine. Volume II (*The Struggle Intensifies*) contains articles pertinent to this campaign
Katcher, Philip, *The American Civil War Source Book* (London, UK, 1996) Brockhampton Press
Konstam, Angus, Campaign Series 124 *Fair Oaks: McClellan's Peninsula Campaign* (Oxford, UK, 2003) Osprey Publishing
Miller, William J. (ed), *The Peninsula Campaign of 1862: Yorktown to the Seven Days* (Campbell, CA, 1993–95) Savas Woodbury. 2 Vols.
Roades, Jeffrey L., *Scapegoat General: The story of Major General Benjamin Huger, CSA* (Hamden, CT,1985). Archon Books
Salmon, John S., *The Official Virginia Civil War Battlefield Guide* (Mechanicsburg, PA, 2001). Stackpole Books
Sears, Stephen W., *George B. McClellan: The Young Napoleon* (New York, NY, 1982) Ticknor & Fields
Sears, Stephen W., *To the Gates of Richmond: The Peninsula Campaign* (New York, NY, 1992). Ticknor & Fields
Swinton, William, *Campaigns of the Army of the Potomac* (Secaucus, NJ, 1988). Blue & Gray Press
Thomason Jr., John W., *Jeb Stuart* (London, 1929). C. Scribners & Sons
Wheeler, Richard, *Sword over Richmond: An eyewitness history of McClellan's Peninsula Campaign* (New York, NY, 1986). Harper & Row
Woodhead, Henry (ed.), *Lee takes Command: From Seven Days to Second Bull Run* (Alexandria, VA, 1984). Time-Life Books "The Civil War" Series

US Government Printing Office, *The War of the Rebellion: A Compilation of the Official Records of the Union and Confederate Armies* (Washington DC, 1889-91). 70 Volumes. Series I. Volume IX is pertinent to this campaign.

INDEX